Religion for Realists

Religion for Realists

Why We All Need the Scientific Study of Religion

SAMUEL L. PERRY

Foreword by
DAVID E. CAMPBELL

OXFORD
UNIVERSITY PRESS

OXFORD
UNIVERSITY PRESS

Oxford University Press is a department of the University of Oxford. It furthers
the University's objective of excellence in research, scholarship, and education
by publishing worldwide. Oxford is a registered trade mark of Oxford University
Press in the UK and certain other countries.

Published in the United States of America by Oxford University Press
198 Madison Avenue, New York, NY 10016, United States of America.

Library of Congress Cataloging-in-Publication Data
Names: Perry, Samuel L., author.
Title: Religion for realists / Samuel L. Perry ; foreword by David E. Campbell.
Description: New York, NY, United States of America : Oxford University Press, [2024] |
Includes bibliographical references and index.
Identifiers: LCCN 2024028529 (print) | LCCN 2024028530 (ebook) | ISBN 9780197672556 (pb) |
ISBN 9780197672549 (hb) | ISBN 9780197672570 (epub) | ISBN 9780197672587
Subjects: LCSH: Religion and sociology. | Religion—Social aspects. | Religion and culture.
Classification: LCC BL60 .P454 2024 (print) | LCC BL60 (ebook) |
DDC 306.6—dc23/eng/20240706
LC record available at https://lccn.loc.gov/2024028529
LC ebook record available at https://lccn.loc.gov/2024028530

DOI: 10.1093/oso/9780197672549.001.0001

Printed by Integrated Books International, United States of America

To my late father, David Perry

Well before the science of religions instituted its method-ological comparisons, men had to create their own idea of what religion is. [...] But because these notions are formed unmethodically, in the comings and goings of life, they cannot be relied on. ... It is not from our preconceptions, passions, or habits that must be consulted for the elements of the definition we need; definition is to be sought from reality itself. Let us set ourselves before this reality.

—Emile Durkheim, *Elementary Forms of Religious Life* ([1912] 1995: 22)

Contents

Foreword

If you are a scholar of something other than religion, this book will convince you that religion matters.

If you are a scholar of religion (or religion *and* something else, such as sociology, political science, or psychology), you presumably are already persuaded that religion is worth studying. This book, however, will convince you that religion should be studied differently than is typically the case.

If you are a member of the "lay" public, you probably do not need to be convinced that religion matters. You might instead be surprised to learn that many scholars need to be persuaded to take religion seriously, given the prominent role that religion plays in many people's lives and society writ large. You may also think that arguments about the study of religion are merely for academics. Rest assured that this book is still for you, as it explains why getting religion right is more than just an academic matter.

For all three of these audiences, *Religion for Realists* makes the case for more, and better, research into religion. That will only happen when more universities and funding agencies recognize the importance of supporting research in religion, which will in turn lead to more scholars who fully embrace the study of religion within many disciplines. But all of this will be in vain if scholars of religion do not translate their research into the vernacular—that is, make their scholarship accessible to the general public beyond the ivory tower.

What would better religion research look like? Samuel Perry makes a compelling case that the study of religion should put belonging first, ahead of believing and behaving. This simple but profound point should seem familiar to many social scientists, as the importance of identity applies to many areas of study. Within my own field of political science, the evidence has long shown that most people's political behavior is not driven by their ideology, but by their partisan identity—an identity that is rooted in social affiliations and affinities. Religion, Perry argues, is much the same. For most people, religious belonging comes first, and from that identity follows both belief and behavior.

Consider the implications of this argument for a society in which belonging is not what it once was. To belong once meant being affiliated with an organized group. In the domain of religion, this is typically a congregation, whether known as a church, parish, synagogue, temple, mosque, or ward. It is in such groups that people develop a sense of trust, and learn how to compromise and cooperate. They form social capital. Over the last generation, such groups—in recent years, congregations especially—have been in decline, and social capital has thus eroded. Today, to belong is more a matter of expressing a personal identity, often through social media, than building community by engaging in face-to-face interaction.

As a result, we get the worst of what James Madison called the mischiefs of faction without the benefit of what Alexis de Tocqueville called the art of association. As Perry notes in the pages to follow, authoritarian leaders are able to exploit people's primal identities, often rooted in religion, to foster exclusion and even violence. A society with low trust and high polarization is ripe for division. In a memorable line, Perry argues that apologists for the far right are very good students of religion—better, in fact, than many religion scholars.

In other words, *Religion for Realists* is about more than whether this or that academic discipline gives religion its due. This book is really a call to arms for a better grasp of how religion does, and does not, help to sustain a democratic society. If we—scholars and the general public alike—do not understand religion, we risk misunderstanding the threat posed by identity-based appeals to those Madisonian impulses within us all. Making democracy work requires getting religion right.

David E. Campbell
University of Notre Dame
Author, *Secular Surge: A New Fault Line in American Politics*

Preface

> True reverence does not consist in declaring a subject, because it is dear to us, to be unfit for free and honest inquiry: far from it! True reverence is shown in treating every subject, however sacred, however dear to us, with perfect confidence; without fear and without favor; with tenderness and love, by all means, but before all, with an unflinching and uncompromising loyalty to truth.
>
> —Friedrich Max Müller, *An Introduction to the Science of Religion* (1870:6)

I assume readers of this book will come to it with different ideas about religion. Many will believe the metaphysical claims of religion—theirs, at least—are true. Many others will deny the reality of any religious claims. And still others will challenge my use of the term "religion" itself as a Western colonial invention, obscuring far more about our social world than it reveals. But I hope we can all agree that the assorted phenomena we typically label "religious," whether they correspond to metaphysical realities or not, are undeniably real in their consequences. The sets of group identities, rituals, symbols, roles, and moral codes we organize under the category "religion" influence the lives of the religious and irreligious alike in myriad ways. And evidence suggests they will continue to do so for the foreseeable future.

Religion for Realists is *not* about debunking religion. And I have no desire whatsoever to propose an alternate, secular religion. I am, in fact, an active participant in a Protestant community myself. Rather, the idea for the title came from the influential book

Democracy for Realists by political scientists Christopher Achen and Larry Bartels (2016). They argue that popular-but-misguided folk theories of how "democracy" works must be reconsidered in light of social scientific evidence. So too, this short book is an argument for why we all need the evidence-based, scientific study of religion—now more than ever. We need it to help us understand how religion *really* works as a social phenomenon.

This book argues that we—by which mean mainly Anglophone Westerners—often misunderstand much about how religion functions. We are steeped in the ambient folk theology of our dominant Anglo-Protestant culture, which is itself sustained by tradition, pastors, pollsters, pop culture, and yes, even we academics at times. Consequently, when we think about "religion" we tend to think about individual belief, doctrines, and the transformative power of individual religious people. On the contrary, religion's importance and power lie more in the deep culture of social norms and identity, the imperatives of population, and the "rules and resources" of social structure.

Insight into these very matters are what the scientific study of religion at its best provides. It has the ability to disrupt many of our pervasive—but erroneous—folk understandings about religion. Science can help us understand how religion works because it helps us understand how we humans work, both as individuals and in groups. And yet, the general public and academic audiences, religious and irreligious alike, are at risk of ignoring what the scientific study of religion can teach us. This book is an argument for why *we all* need the scientific study of religion now and a practical roadmap for ensuring that its insights are widely available, accessible, and impactful.

I've attempted to write this book for three audiences.

The first is simply interested nonspecialists, whether they identify as religious or not. If this describes you, I want you to understand how insights from the scientific study of religion help us make sense not only of how religion works in our world, but also how our world works in general. I want you to learn something about religion and all the things it touches, which as it turns out is just about everything. But I also want you to start thinking more in terms of unconscious bias and group loyalties than self-conscious beliefs; more about fertility rates, cohorts, and immigration than doctrines; and at least as much about social structures as about human agency. With that knowledge I want you to be better equipped to evaluate the claims made by prophets, pastors, pundits, pollsters, and politicians, who are all too eager to shape your understanding of religion in exchange for your devotion, attention, money, or vote. Science is knowledge, and knowledge is freedom. For that reason the scientific study of religion, though limited and imperfect, is liberating. It is well worth your time and, I hope, your trust.

Because I've written the book to be short and accessible to this first audience, I've placed a large amount of material in the endnotes. That content includes many citations to work that goes into much greater depth and complexity than I am able to do in the text itself. These studies provide a wealth of information, and I encourage interested readers to familiarize themselves with all the fascinating work being done on these topics. Due to space constraints, I have also placed all the tables for the book's many figures on my department website currently hosted by the University of Oklahoma. Readers are more than welcome to double-check those numbers or reproduce figures yourself using the available data.

The second audience is academics in the secular academy whose life's work is to understand our world and disseminate knowledge to benefit the first audience, and beyond. There is a curiously persistent mismatch between religion's relevance in human social life and its place in the academy. And that situation is worsening. Today, religious studies departments are fighting for their lives. Social science advisors practically (and sometimes explicitly) forbid their graduate students from studying religion for fear that it will make their employment prospects even dimmer than they already are.

I want to convince you the neglect of religion by social scientists is a problem worth addressing.

Religion is relevant, and increasingly so. Authoritarian leaders who already understand quite well how religion works are emerging to threaten stable democracies, including our own. They do this by seeking to stoke conflict based on group identity, manipulate population dynamics, and arrange systems to advantage their cultural in-groups forever. The scientific study of religion helps us understand not only these realities but also dozens of other critical social processes. Budgets are tight all over. But we still have choices about what areas we hire for, fund, promote, and reward, and religion should be among the top choices. When we refuse to recognize this, we're revealing more about ourselves than benign disinterest in religion. We're showing a malignant anti-religion bias that should be extirpated until the margins are clear.

The third audience is my tribe of religion scholars. Regardless of our discipline or methodological approach, the evidence-based study of religion must improve in the areas of transparency, accountability, and accessibility. I have no intention of championing quantitative methods over more qualitative or humanistic methods. But I will argue that all of us should consider why many Americans don't trust our work and how our antiquated systems of quality control and dissemination may be complicit. Beyond merely valuing our own livelihoods, we have an obligation—to the deeply religious, the resolutely irreligious, and people somewhere in between—to produce research that merits and engenders trust. In addition, we must ensure that our audiences receive information in a way that is not only accessible, but delivered to them proactively. I argue that implementing open science principles can help us improve the credibility and reach of our work. This will help us better fulfill the promise of science.

Acknowledgments

I wrote this book during what has been the busiest time in my personal and professional life to date. In case readers hadn't noticed, it's been a hectic time to study American religion and politics. And in the year leading up to finishing this book I've been doing interviews, podcasts, op-eds, and flying around the country multiple times a month to speak, all while maintaining a full teaching load and trying to be a considerate husband to a working spouse and a hands-on dad to three wonderfully energetic children. I've loved nearly every minute of it. But this schedule has made book-writing difficult. Thanks are in order for making it possible.

First, let me stress the people I thank are in no way to blame for any shortcomings of this book, nor should they be understood as personally endorsing the arguments. In fact, some will strongly disagree. Regardless, I'm so grateful for their insights and encouragement.

Thanks to Theo Caldarara, my longtime editor at Oxford University Press, for humoring me with this one, and for his patience during this busy season.

Thanks also go to my students. I'm extremely grateful to my doctoral students Joshua T. Davis, who recently slayed the academic job market as a crime and race specialist who "also studies religion" (wink, wink), and Elizabeth E. McElroy, now a post-doc at Indiana University and for whom the sky's the limit. I'm grateful for their friendship and help in collecting some of the survey experiment data used in Chapter 2.

Thanks to my mentors and cohort of early-career scholars in the Young Scholars in American Religion program through the Center for the Study of Religion & American Culture. You've all taught me so much about religion scholarship, particularly as you've helped me get outside my subfield of sociology to consider insights from history and religious studies. I'm grateful for your brilliant feedback and friendship.

At the University of Oklahoma, I'm always grateful for my department colleagues and particularly for my longtime chair, Loretta Bass. Loretta has been a tremendous advocate and advisor during my time at the university and I owe her a ton. Enjoy the well-deserved break, Loretta.

Lastly, I want to thank my family. Thanks to my three extraordinary kids, Ryan, Beau, and Whitman, for regularly asking about the book, if only to express their exasperation that it wasn't finished yet. You each bring joy and purpose to my life more than any book or job. As always, thanks to my wife, Jill. You've been a constant encouragement, both during my career and especially during this busy season. I owe you forever.

I dedicate this book to my father, David Perry, who died in 2020. Other than my wife, Dad was my best friend and greatest encouragement. I miss him the most when I get a promotion, win some award, or finish a big project like this book. He'd have been proud regardless, but he got so visibly excited when I shared fun professional news, telling him was always tremendously satisfying. Thanks go to my mom for her love and for carrying Dad's mantle in regularly asking about work stuff and being tickled at good news.

Introduction

Real, But Different

In these our days it is almost impossible to speak of religion at all, without giving offense either on the right or the left. With some, religion seems too sacred a subject for scientific treatment; with others it stands on a level with alchemy and astrology, as a mere tissue of errors or hallucinations, far beneath the notice of the man of science.

> —Friedrich Max Müller, *An Introduction to the Science of Religion* (1870:4)

The question of the desirability of an objective study of religion is even more controversial than the question of its possibility. There are few major subjects about which men know so little, yet feel so certain. . . . At one extreme it is held that one's received religion has all the necessary thinking already embodied in it. At the other, religion is dismissed as insufficiently important to command the resources of scholarship.

> —J. Milton Yinger, *The Scientific Study of Religion* (1970:2–3).

On a recent 14-hour flight from Los Angeles to Sydney, desperate to pass the time, I began scrolling the hundreds of movie options on

Religion for Realists. Samuel L. Perry, Oxford University Press. © Oxford University Press 2024.
DOI: 10.1093/oso/9780197672549.003.0001

the seatback in front of me. I've been flying long distances a lot recently and this ritual has convinced me the airlines must employ an algorithm that works in reverse. They only seem to offer me movies that I'd never want to watch. On this occasion, however, I was thrilled to see each of the Indiana Jones movies available. I grew up on the original trilogy, covering the whip-wielding, Nazi-punching exploits of archeology Professor Henry "Indiana" Jones Jr., played by Harrison Ford. It had been years since I'd seen any of them. So I cracked open my Twizzler stash and settled in for an Indiana Jones marathon.

As I watched the movies, now approaching a decade as a professional sociologist of religion, something new stuck out to me. There was an aspect of Dr. Jones's world that I found almost as uncanny as his supernatural adventures—yet strangely familiar. What struck me as so remarkable is that not only are all of the gods Indiana Jones encounters absolutely real and incredibly powerful, but almost everything we learn about how they operate contradicts the central teachings of Abrahamic faiths that dominate our Western understanding, particularly Christianity. Yet we see no evidence that anybody knows or cares, including his students, university colleagues, other scholars in his field, or the wider public.

In iconic scenes that filled the nightmares of my childhood, Indy and his associates witness Yahweh melt Nazi faces off, the Hindu goddess Kali facilitate the disemboweling of live humans, and decoy Holy Grails turn men into desiccated corpses. Put yourself in these movies for a moment. What we learn in Indiana's adventures changes everything for religious and irreligious humans alike. Everything we think we know about religion in the West is turned upside down. Monotheism? A myth. The gods of Judaism, Hinduism, and Christianity are apparently all real and seem to care far more about ritual impurity than morality or faith. The world should know! Get Indiana Jones booked on all the shows!

And it should go without saying that the academic contributions of these discoveries would be the most important in history. The

Harvards, Princetons, and Oxfords of the world should be lining up. Dr. Jones should be able to name his price and work anywhere he wishes. Funders should be at the ready. Such earth-shattering findings would immediately transform our entire world, and Dr. Jones would become our most celebrated, sought-after, and well-funded scholar.

But here's another consistent theme in all the movies, even the more recent ones that fast-forward decades ahead in his career: nobody knows or cares. Even though everything Westerners thought they knew about religion is wrong, none of Indy's findings have transformed anything about how people approach religion or their world, either among the general public or in the academy. Indy lives most of his life in obscurity; his job as an academic is drab; his work is unacknowledged and poorly funded.[1]

Outrageous? Absolutely.

Unbelievable? Not if you also study religion.

Why This Book?

Like Indiana Jones, I know "the gods" are real. I don't necessarily mean real in the ontological sense—that they actually exist and act in the world. But rather I know religion is among the most powerful and pervasive forces in the world. I know "the gods" are real because the norms, traditions, myths, and roles premised on their realness continue to shape the lives of billions. Or, to quote some of the earliest sociologists, "if men define situations as real, they are real in their consequences."[2] This is true whether we are religious or not and regardless of whether academics like me recognize it.

But as we learn from Indiana Jones, the evidence suggests "the gods" don't operate the way we often think they do. We've gotten religion wrong, largely because we (yes, including Western academics) tend to think with very Anglo-Protestant-centric conceptions and folk theologies rather than with evidence from the social sciences about how human beings actually think and behave. By "Anglo-Protestant" I mainly mean our pervasive assumptions that (1) personal faith is the driver of religious behavior and ideas or doctrines are religion's foundational materials (Protestant) and (2) individual actors and their choices are masters of their own religious futures (Anglo or Anglo American). I will argue this conception of religion, at least to the extent we prioritize it, is empirically dead wrong in each respect. And our failure to change our understanding of religion in light of what social science teaches us— perhaps due to lack of awareness or outright refusal—is frankly as consequential as the general public in Indiana Jones's world going about life oblivious to the realities he witnesses.

This book is a short argument about how the scientific study of religion should transform our dominant understandings of religion in the West, some reasons why it has failed to do so, and what must be adjusted in the future to change that.

I have no intention of empirically debunking Protestantism or religion generally. I am, in fact, a lifelong Protestant, in a family of Protestants, with a Protestant seminary education. Yet dominant Anglo-Protestant assumptions about what motivates human beings (faith), what directs the futures of religious communities and broader societies (ideas or doctrines, often found in sacred texts), and the emphasis they place on individual agency are largely wrong. Not biblically or morally wrong. I won't speak to either of those issues. But they *are* empirically wrong. Instead, I'll argue the scientific study of religion helps us understand that humans are in greater part driven by the more fundamentally cognitive "deep culture" of social norms, identities, and loyalties; societies are transformed less by moral ideas or doctrines than by discernible transitions in human populations; and our agency, to an extent we may resent recognizing, is powerfully shaped by social structure—the layers of laws, policies, formal roles, material resources, and institutions in which we live our lives.

We need a religion for realists. That's *not* a declaration in favor of secular humanism or some other replacement religion.[3] I mean intelligent citizens, whether they're religious or not, need to incorporate into their mental models an understanding of how religion works that's based on empirical data, something the scientific study of religion can at its best provide. But that brings me to another reason why I've written this book.

This book emerges out of a tremendous personal and professional frustration I've endured for over a decade. This hair-pulling vexation is aimed primarily at members of my own proud guild, the secular academy, and specifically, the social sciences. Some aspects of my exasperation have evolved as I've transitioned from graduate student, to job market candidate, to junior scholar, to tenured associate, and now a full professor with my former doctoral students out in the world. But my feelings have only intensified, from initial bewilderment upon beginning graduate school to the kind of rage that drives one to, well, write a whole book.

Put simply, something else about Indiana Jones's professional life struck me as all too familiar: the fact that those of us who study religion professionally know what the vast majority of human beings on this planet know—religion matters. The identities, traditions, practices, objects, spaces, and institutions we call "religious" powerfully shape human life everywhere on this planet. Yet paradoxically, the secular academy, and the social sciences in particular, continue to deprioritize or ignore this most fundamental and pervasive of human experiences. I'm not remotely the first scholar to make that observation.[4] But the situation may be getting worse. Religious Studies Departments are shrinking or closing. Sociology, psychology, and political science departments almost never hire for religion specifically. The National Science Foundation and the National Institutes of Health rarely fund it. Without minimizing the importance of issues like environmental degradation, racial inequality, opioid addiction, mass incarceration, mental health, global pandemics, gun violence, and the future of liberal democracies, religion not only matters in its own right, but it is also connected to all the other areas we already deem worthy of study.

Beyond my plea to the general public to consider a "religion for realists," I wrote this book as a declaration to my colleagues in the secular academy, and particularly within the social sciences. I write to tell them, bluntly, to wake up. Religion doesn't go away when we stop researching it and writing about it. Instead, other voices gladly rush in to fill that vacuum and tell the world everything they think they need to know about religion. And many of these voices will belong to charlatans, partisan shills, and demagogues. Due to a combination of wishful thinking, elitist contempt, prejudice, and discomfort around religious issues, we are ceding the field to pollsters, pastors, grifters, and authoritarians. And we're missing our opportunity to make a real contribution.

Why Definitions of Religion Matter: And Why They Don't

This book argues that religion matters, but we've got it largely wrong, and we need the scientific study of religion to fix that. But what do I mean by "religion"? Definitions of religion are as abundant as they are contentious. And it shouldn't be surprising that we're more likely to appreciate definitions of "religion" that suit our identities, ideological commitments, community norms, and the tools we have on hand to understand it.[5]

Social scientists, for example, are often partial to defining "religion" as traditional beliefs and practices relative to supposed superhuman powers. (Scholars often say super*human* rather than super*natural*, because the idea is not that such powers are *un*natural, but that they are believed to exist in a reality inaccessible to humans and to shape reality in ways humans cannot.[6]) This approach often suits us professionally and, for many, personally. Professionally, we can easily measure "belief, belonging, and behavior," or more specifically, how many people indicate on surveys that they hold certain beliefs, identify with some group, or engage in some practice. And thus, there's something we can offer to the conversation. Moreover, as I'll show later, social scientists tend to be a rather secular-minded bunch and defining religion in this particular way allows them to bask in the satisfaction of knowing that religion is clearly on the wane in the Western world. A vast amount of polling evidence suggests that belief in god or gods, religious affiliation, and worship attendance are all steadily declining in the United States just as it has throughout Europe and Canada. If that's pretty much all there is to religion, then religion may slide into irrelevance sometime in the near future.[7]

But if we define "religion" using something far broader like Emile Durkheim's "beliefs and practices relative to sacred things," that changes the game. First, it becomes more difficult to measure religion, which is annoying for social scientists like myself. But more than this, those who are pro-religion can not only take satisfaction knowing we're all religious in some way, they can also draw political implications. If Homo sapiens are a religious species, if myth-making, god-projecting, and group-sacralizing are all hardwired into us somehow, then a purely secular society doesn't just put us at odds with our very nature, it's impossible. And I don't mean to suggest that this understanding of religion has no secular or progressive proponents. Self-identified atheists and liberal public intellectuals like Jonathan Haidt and Yuval Noah Harari promote definitions of religion so expansive that they include devotion to sports teams and communism.[8] Yet the "everyone is religious in some way" understanding of religion is also currently being leveraged by American Christian nationalists to justify their quest for political power. The reasoning goes, "If there's no such thing as 'secular government,' and every regime is 'religious' in some way, then it's either our religion in charge or yours."[9] This doesn't mean their definition is wrong. But the appeal of certain definitions is as subject to motivated reasoning as religion itself.

Still other scholars challenge attempts to define "religion" at all as a hopelessly colonial project. A brilliant young scholar of secularism, Joseph Blankholm, has proposed that "religion," in the American context at least, often means little more than "analogous to Christianity." I think he's exactly right and, as I'll explain below, this is precisely why a more systematic, evidence-based consideration of religion is so necessary. Blankholm documents that even many self-consciously secular Americans often behave "religiously." That is, they often embrace patterns of group participation and ideas of purity and pollution that look very "religious" if by that we mean "analogous to Christianity" (which we in the West most often do unless we intentionally try to do otherwise). This fact often provokes conversation and contention within the American secular community. How should they live as secular people in a society that has been so indelibly shaped by Christian language, traditions, identities, and symbols? What should they keep? What should they avoid?[10]

Blankholm and other scholars in the "critical religion" camp offer a vital insight in that our academic conversations about religion are often better served by paying attention to how certain groups think about "religion" and behave "religiously" within their own context. What if, as religion scholar Ann Taves asks, we didn't try to define "religion" in its essence but focused more on *why* certain people, places, or experiences are "deemed religious" and *how* those definitions serve to produce or *re*produce certain social arrangements?[11]

As a social scientist, I'll proceed from the understanding that "religion" is fundamentally groupish. That is because Homo sapiens are groupish. Consequently, calling something "religious" means nothing apart from how groups understand it according to their social context. Do you think Donald Trump is "religious"? Even more so than Joe Biden? Most Republicans and many white evangelicals think so. And most Democrats and Black Protestants vehemently disagree. And each can be right, according to how they understand the term "religious" within their own social context.[12] In fact, among numerous reasons the scientific study of religion is more important now than ever is the growing overlap between various group identities in the United States and elsewhere. These overlaps mean that religious identities and language increasingly tell us more about individuals' political and cultural leanings now than they have in modern history.[13]

But religion isn't just something that inheres within individuals or our daily interactions. In fact, one of the critical contributions of the scientific study of religion, and in particular my academic discipline of sociology, is that religion is also part of the social *structure*: our laws, writings, buildings, leadership, and the distribution of resources. That's one of the reasons it remains so powerful. Religion is codified in our expectations, policies, and even physical surroundings in ways that influence even the nonreligious. That understanding of religion is seldom included informal definitions of religion, but a "religion for realists" requires it.[14]

For the purposes of this book, "religion" represents whatever subjective and objective realities human beings and their communities perceive and relate to as "religious." Subjective realities include identities, beliefs, values, emotions, subconscious cognitions, and the experience of the physical world. Objective realities include stable patterns of social behavior and organization, laws, texts, objects, materials, and spaces. The scientific study of religion is *the systematic, evidence-based approach to understanding these subjective and objective realities of religion with an eye toward expanding practical knowledge for humankind.* Notice I didn't say anything about quantifying religious phenomena. That can certainly be part of it. But my colleagues in Religious Studies and Anthropology can rest assured I don't mean "scientific" as a synonym for "survey research." To the extent we are employing a systematic, evidence-based approach toward the goal of expanding practical knowledge about all-things-religious, that's the science I'm talking about.

But what exactly does the scientific study of religion contribute that's so important? And what is preventing us from benefiting from those insights? Though I've sketchily previewed some key points already, here let me clarify my overall argument.

My Arguments

Over the first four chapters, I focus on three pervasive misconceptions about how religion works. I also present ways in which the evidence-based, scientific study of religion reveals "religion for realists." Religion scholar Joseph Blankholm was certainly correct when he said we in the West often say "religion" to mean little more than "analogous to Christianity." But I would go a little further and say "religion" in the United States means something like "analogous to Anglo-Protestantism." For all the inaccuracies in the whitewashed historical accounts of white Christian nationalists, they do speak truth in some regards. Specifically, they are correct when they argue our laws and culture have been dominated by Anglo-Protestants and Anglo-Protestantism, often historically with the very explicit intention of privileging both. Anglo-Protestants have largely been our leaders, by their own design. And Anglo-Protestantism, in combination with our unique admixture of enlightenment ideals and immigrant cultures, has shaped our dominant folk understanding of religion and how religion works.

What exactly is that understanding? Table I.1 presents three domains of how we think of religion's *primary* cognitive force

Table I.1. Primary Operant in Religion According to Anglo-Protestant Tradition vs. Reality

Domain	Anglo-Protestant Tradition	Reality
Cognitive Force	Beliefs (Faith)	Social Identity and Norms
Growth Factor	Ideas (Doctrines)	Population Dynamics
Change Agent	Individuals (Obedience)	Social Structure

(what orients and drives people psychologically), growth factor (what directs or shapes the trajectory of religion in society), and change agent. I argue there are three theological assumptions that reflect a specific, Americanized, Anglo-Protestant conception of how religion and society operate together. None of them are necessarily inherent in Christianity itself, and are certainly not inherent in most other world religions. But they are manifestly dominant in this context. As an alternative, I argue that the social sciences reveal three operant factors that more accurately capture reality. These three social realities are all interrelated, but I will give each its own chapter.

From Beliefs to Social Identities and Norms

The first pervasive-but-mistaken religious assumption is perhaps the most central to the Anglo-Protestant self-understanding. I anticipate it will be the most difficult to reconsider, despite its being demonstrably untrue. This is that human behavior is oriented around and driven by complexes of theological beliefs or what we might call "worldviews." We may or may not be consciously aware of these beliefs, but they nevertheless can be influenced through religious activities that target them: things like preaching, interpersonal persuasion, and reading. This is an assumption grounded in the Anglo-Protestant theological tradition, which dominates our understanding of how to interpret human behaviors and the strategies by which we attempt to transform human societies.[15]

Why do atheists and Black Protestants vote for Democrats? Why do evangelicals oppose expanding transgender rights? Why don't seculars go to church? Why don't religious conservatives want to pass legislation that will restrict gun rights? And why do they support the death penalty? Why do different religious groups favor dealing with the poor in different ways? The dominant

Anglo-Protestant paradigm is that people are operating on the basis of semicoherent and semiconscious "worldviews" or "beliefs" about moral authority and ultimate truth. Thus, the engine of religious motivation and even identification with religion itself is oriented around the presence or absence of "faith." We commonly designate religious people in the United States as "believers" and "people of faith." TV shows about non-Christian religions have names like "Believer" and "Islands of Faith." In fact, "religion" and "faith" are often used interchangeably. Even our designation for the supposedly most self-consciously irreligious persons in our culture—agnostics and atheists—speaks mostly to their skepticism toward or rejection of faith in superhuman deities. Thus, as Blankholm points out, even the seculars find their lives oriented around analogues to Christianity. They are, as he puts it, "living in religion's remainder."[16]

But should rational (by that I mean, conscious, reasoning) belief be the center of the conversation? Is belief really the driver of religious activity? Is belief really what makes people "religious" or "irreligious"? Religious studies scholars have long argued otherwise, and social science agrees.[17] What really orients our lives and activities, and something I'll argue is more to the core of religion itself, is our subjective identification with and loyalty to social groups. Social identities, representing something far more cognitive and primal than our theological beliefs, are more often what drive the ship. Formal theological beliefs, by contrast, are more often the claims we make to signal our social identities, the stories we use to make sense of our circumstances, and the justifications we cite to explain our behavior to others. To use moral psychologist Jonathan Haidt's famous metaphor, our social identities and group loyalties are what drive the "elephant," the reactive part of our brain, which acts on the basis of intuition, gut reactions, and a deeper socialization. Theological beliefs supply mental maps and language for the "rider" (our rational faculties) who may occasionally be successful in redirecting the elephant, but is most often simply the social translator for the elephant, helping others understand its behavior using socially approved explanations.

Why is this important to know? In a world where our religious identities are increasingly subordinated to our partisan loyalties and ideological identities, our religious identities are growing more synonymous with political and ethnocultural tribes. On the one hand, this serves to drive religious change. For example, culturally progressive, nominally religious Americans are increasingly embracing an "unaffiliated" religious identity that fits their political and ideological identity. But this also ratchets up political conflict, as secular and religious belief systems increasingly justify widening political divisions. Research shows certain combinations of religious beliefs, now operating from an "us vs. them" framework based on partisanship, are amplifying partisan conflict to Cosmic proportions, while also justifying the most extreme measures to defeat one's enemies, who are aligned with Satan.[18]

From Ideas to Population Dynamics

There is a second pervasive misunderstanding about religion's "realness" that social science corrects. This is the misconception that religious growth and decline are primarily about the transformative potential of ideas. This is again at the core of the Anglo-Protestant understanding, but one that New Atheists themselves often affirm in principle: religion isn't just about sincere faith, but faith in ideas. Thus, the debate centers around who has the *right* ideas, principally the right ideas about God, but also the right ideas about humanity, the family, morality, and politics. According to this assumption, it is *those* religions and their nations, those who align their ideas with God's revealed truth, who emerge victorious in numbers and prosperity. And it is those religions and those nations that align their ideas with worldliness and idolatry who shrivel up or collapse under the weight of their own decadence. Numbers and prosperity, in other words, are taken as a sign of God's affirmation that you've gotten the ideas right.

This misconception gives rise to two opposite orientations to the reality of populations, one that refuses to recognize its influence and another that hopes in vain to change it. The first orientation stresses conversionism without regard for demographic realities, while the other recognizes the vital importance of demographic realities, but still believes religious groups can manufacture demographic majorities by convincing the right populations with the right ideas.

On the one hand, social science suggests religious growth and decline has always been more about the causes and consequences of population change than whatever theological ideas are being propagated. Protestant? Catholic? Muslim? The theological specifics haven't been so important as the realities of fertility, mortality, and immigration. Take the United States, for example. Contrary to what many of us were taught growing up, social science now tells us that much of our contemporary ethnoreligious makeup is the result of fertility differentials and immigration flows.

But some deeply religious Americans are, in fact, very cognizant of the importance of demography. In fact, it's becoming fairly clear that as those on the Christian Right are losing confidence in their ability to persuade secular Americans to embrace conservative Christianity (probably not an inaccurate assessment), they are placing a larger portion of their bets on demographic victory. I'll show, however, that even this idea betrays a misunderstanding of the facts on the ground. Conservative Christians, like all other Americans, are implicated in the broader structural changes that are both driving down fertility across the board and resulting in more citizens in the Western world embracing secularism from birth or as adults. That brings us to the final major correction the scientific study of religion provides.

From Individual Obedience to Social Structure

This last misconception about religion is one we Americans in particular tend to hold onto because it is not only deeply embedded within the Anglo-Protestant tradition, but within what it means to be an American. Put simply, we tend to think of "religion" and religious change as something we as individuals and groups control. Thus, we tend to think that whether religion goes in one direction or another, whether it grows or declines, depends on choices we make to believe and do the right things.

But the evidence requires us to adjust our paradigm. Many of the religious changes we have been and will continue to witness around the world—including demographic patterns and transitions in social identity—are related to social structures.

Think about the decline of religious affiliation and practice in the United States and Western Europe. Is this primarily the result of people abandoning religious "worldviews," switching from one set of ideas to another? If that were the case, then religious people could take stock of what competing ideas took hold of such populations, and figure out what they could do to make religious faith more appealing intellectually and emotionally. They could get organized, build relationships, take apologetics courses, and develop reputations as loving neighbors and citizens. But in reality, these long-term trends toward secularism are downstream of a variety of structural factors related to economics, politics, and family life.

Analyses of global secularization patterns indicate that levels of religious identification and participation are powerfully interconnected to economic and political stability, the money governments invest in education, whether the state privileges specific religious groups, the structure of families, the presence of religious competitors, and many other factors. And those broader structural phenomena are maintained by federal and state laws, international treaties, multinational corporations, multiple layers of institutions, and the social dynamics of life in complex societies. Changing them may already be beyond the scope of what highly-motivated-but-shrinking religious communities can accomplish.

What is more, we find ourselves facing the reality that the broader structural phenomena that contribute to religion's decline involve political and social arrangements *we dare not change.* Meta-analytic evidence from hundreds of studies shows that government investment in education increases economic growth. But studies also suggest those same expenditures help explain falling church attendance rates. Religious liberty is a core national value that a growing proportion of Americans support, one that has increasingly become institutionalized since America's founding. Yet numerous studies now show religious diversity is accelerating religious decline. Social welfare spending not only supports needy populations, it also boosts marriage rates. But it's also associated with religious decline, possibly because the state replaces churches as a source of support, or perhaps because it decouples marriage and fertility.[19]

So which should we abandon? Do we halt government spending on education and potentially forsake economic growth? Should we rethink religious liberty for all and become authoritarian Christian nationalists? Do we further cut social welfare spending and leave the elderly, poor, and sick to hope that the rapidly diminishing number of churches fill the gap?

Now More than Ever

Taken together, we see emerging and interrelated trends in social identity, populations, and social structure are creating a situation in which religion is at a crossroads. The implications for religious Americans should be clear. But this is also where the urgency of this book becomes clearer for irreligious Americans and secular academics. There are already certain groups of Americans who have embraced a "religion for realists." They understand religion in terms of identity, not faith; demography, not ideas; and structure, not individual piety. They are right-wing authoritarian ethnonationalists. They have analogues all over the world—in Hungary, Brazil, Italy, France, Russia, India, Myanmar, and the Middle East. And by their own admission, they would gladly change structural factors in order to regain what they feel is lost. The American iterations of this phenomenon would, for example, abandon or replace public education to bolster the "Christian worldview," restrict religious liberty to revive Christian supremacy, and diminish welfare spending to recenter the Christian church as the source of social welfare and re-establish the traditional patriarchal family. The social scientific study of religion reveals their game plan.

In the last two chapters, I propose changes that would promote the scientific study of religion and make the important insights it provides more accessible to concerned Americans. I don't lay blame at the feet of the general public. Rather, I propose we in the academy must accept responsibility for meeting the need.

The first part of my argument here is that secular academics, and particularly those in the social sciences, are not only guilty of benign disinterest in religion but also outright prejudice against those who study it. We are more likely to suspect religion specialists of "me-search"—of focusing on topics that are personal to them—and of being conservative and religious. This leads to a downgrading of the very scholars and research we need in order to inform the public of critical changes taking place. But it also reveals a failure to live up to our own scientific standards of ruthlessly scrutinizing our own biases and systematically addressing them. We are not without choices in the sort of work we hire for and reward. When we consistently choose not to hire for and promote the scientific study of religion, we're revealing that we have not dealt with our own biases, to the detriment of those whom we should serve.[20]

The second part of my argument is that social scientists of religion must earn the trust of the general public. Certainly there

are those who will always distrust academics who critique falla-
cious reasoning and debunk cherished beliefs with data. But evidence suggests even religious Americans have a high regard for
science itself, and that scientists can earn greater trust by leaning
into the open science movement, committing in practical ways to
increasing accountability, transparency, and accessibility. This not
only demonstrates the rigor and relevance of our work to other
academics but also, more importantly, better fulfills the promise of
science itself—benefiting all citizens. And at the end of the day, that
is the goal of this book.

But first, I need to establish a key premise for the chapters
ahead. Just how do we know our conceptions about religion are
*mis*conceptions? And how pervasive are they? I'll showcase plenty
of evidence from the social sciences in chapters 2–4, but in the following chapter I set the stage with a case from my own research to
illustrate the problem.

1

We Were All Wrong

Anglo-Protestant Misconceptions

One of the most fascinating puzzles in the world to me is the relationship between religion and self-sacrifice on behalf of one's group. And I don't just mean suicide bombing and literally drinking Kool-Aid at Jonestown. I also mean the mundane, everyday sacrifices people make to accomplish "religious" goals. What is it about religion that drives otherwise comfortable people to collectively risk money, convenience, and in some cases even personal safety? Why do some endure heartache, material insecurity, and professional stigma? I obsessed over this puzzle so much that for my dissertation at the University of Chicago I determined to study religious Americans who were engaging in risky or costly forms of activism.

But whom to study? Around 2011, I heard talk of a movement among evangelical Christians to promote what we could call "high-risk" and "high-cost" forms of adoption and foster care in local churches—what was then called the "Christian orphan care movement." Certainly, adopting a child is personally rewarding. But personal reward wasn't the going narrative about these adoptions. Evangelical families, I was told, were signing up en masse to raise funds and try to adopt as many children as possible, both domestically and overseas. Many were apparently eager to adopt children with physical or behavioral special needs. I grew up in an evangelical family with adopted African American sisters and so this case study of collective action held a particular fascination for me. But I actually first learned about this movement from its critics.[1]

Religion for Realists. Samuel L. Perry, Oxford University Press. © Oxford University Press 2024.
DOI: 10.1093/oso/9780197672549.003.0002

Starting around 2007 and continuing on up to 2013, progressive journalists and adoptee-rights activists were troubled by the prospect of conservative Christians missionary-adopting. They churned out scores of articles about the menacing "evangelical adoption crusade." By their account, thousands of evangelical "serial adopters," driven by pro-life commitments and The Great Commission, were tirelessly organizing, funding, and advocating a "new Gospel of adoption" that was being carried out worldwide.[2] And this wasn't a baseless accusation, because the positive version of this narrative was being promulgated by movement leaders and authors. The Christian Alliance for Orphans, a coalition of Christian adoption agencies and advocacy ministries, proudly touted "what *Christianity Today* called the 'burgeoning Christian orphan care movement.'"[3] Leaders repeated tales of how Christian families reduced the number of children waiting for adoption from Colorado's foster care system by more than half in 2 years. Authors cited how "an increasing number of families are pursuing adoption . . . in response to God's call," and "Thousands of Christians have discovered God's heart for the orphan."[4] And as I discovered myself, there was no shortage of Christian adoptive families who'd tell you at the first chance, "We felt the calling to adopt because of the gospel."

The narrative was clear and consistent from devout insiders and critical outsiders alike: sincere religious faith was driving individual behavior; some rediscovered "theology of adoption" was directing their sincerity into effective actions; and this was largely a grassroots, bottom-up phenomenon. The Christian orphan care movement, in other words, was a story about the power of religious faith, ideas, and individuals. Faith was propelling sacrificial obedience. God's ideas about what true Christianity looks like were transforming hearts. And those transformed hearts were transforming society, one child at a time. Nobody questioned this storyline; the only debate was whether the impact was for better or for worse.

But here's where the story gets weird. They were all wrong. Nothing was changing. When I looked at the numbers, there was no evidence of a Christian adoption crusade. There still isn't, in fact. Specifically, there is no evidence that Christians have moved the needle on adoption and foster care numbers at all, no evidence that Christians' behaviors have changed in response to all the books, conferences, and sermons. Certainly some change happened anecdotally, at the level of a few individuals, but not to any sort of scale.

How could everyone be so wrong? Were these secular journalists and Christian leaders lying? Absolutely not. Is this an example of "religion" itself failing in its goals? Again, no.

The difference between what outside observers and participants described in the orphan care movement and what the empirical data actually tell us reveals pervasive misconceptions about how religion actually works in real life. Not only did these misconceptions extend beyond devout Christian circles to include journalists, academics, and pollsters, but these groups likewise contributed to the confusion. In the orphan care movement as elsewhere, these misconceptions boil down to the dominant Anglo-Protestant folk assumption that "religion" is about the interplay of faith, ideas, and agency.

Why Religious Narratives Can Mislead

I met Brian and Lauren Davis in the course of my research. I needed to better understand the goals and motivations of people who adopt and foster children. So I spent several years interviewing hundreds of Christians and non-Christians, activists and otherwise, who'd been active in adoption or foster care. Brian and Lauren Davis were among the lovely couples who shared their adoption story with me.

A year or so after our conversation in their Dallas home, I stumbled on an adoption ministry website featuring Brian and Lauren among several video testimonials. Curious to see how they would articulate their adoption journey to Christian viewers thinking about adoption, I clicked on the video. After introducing his family, Brian explained "how God brought our family together."

> We felt the calling to adopt because of the gospel. The gospel tells us that because of what Christ did for us, that we can have salvation. And then that Christ tells us at the end of Matthew that we are to go and take the gospel with us, and we thought one of the best ways to do that, one of the ways that we felt called to go and share the gospel is to adopt. And to bring our child that God had for us into our home and to share the gospel with [that child].[5]

Pretty clear, right? According to Brian, he and Lauren were compelled by faith in the gospel. Adoption, in their thinking, was also one of the best ways they could obey Jesus's command to share the gospel with others.

Almost every evangelical adoptive couple I interviewed spoke this way initially. So did almost all the evangelical leaders writing books about adoption. So did their critics, based largely on the testimonies of couples like Brian and Lauren and books written by evangelical leaders.

But there was one discrepancy that kept popping up. When I probed deeper into the stories of most adoptive couples I interviewed, their initial interest in adopting didn't begin with the gospel or the Great Commission, but with fertility struggles. Brian and Lauren fit that description too. In our interview, Lauren recounted that doctors diagnosed her with endometriosis in high school and told her she might not ever have children, a fact that Brian learned when they began dating in college. Going into marriage, both knew adoption was likely their only option for children.

This discrepancy in accounts appeared so often I began to expect it. Christian couples would tell me something like "We adopted because we're following God's heart for the orphan," or "We've been adopted by God through Christ, so we feel called to adopt children as a way to live out the gospel." Some of them even said it was a commitment to a Christian pro-life ethic. And to be clear, I think they had come to believe those narratives when they recounted them. After all, they'd each shared their story dozens of times before on fundraising websites, in front of churches, or to curious journalists. But when I would press further and ask if they'd ever tried to have children biologically, they'd almost invariably reply "Oh yeah, we tried for years. We took hormones and several rounds of in vitro, but it never took." This was also the story of most evangelical authors whose books were advocating Christian adoption and foster care as "Plan A" rather than "Plan B." Big names like Paul and Robin Pennington (the founders of the orphan care movement), Russell Moore, David Platt, and numerous other leaders and authors all described to me or in their own books their struggles with infertility.

None of this is to accuse any of these families of hypocrisy or lying. That explanation is, in fact, too simplistic. Too naive. These families were indeed driven to adopt, but not *initially* because of some unwavering faith in the "theology of adoption" or "the Great Commission" or "the gospel." What drove them to adopt was something deeper, more foundational to how these persons were raised, more central to their understanding of what their lives should look like, but was nevertheless thwarted by physical barriers. What drove them was a combination of social identity and group norms, in this case, the (sometimes unspoken, sometimes explicit) understanding that "people like us" have children and are defined by parenthood. Polling data show conservative Christians are historically among the nation's leaders in fertility. They also tend to have a higher ideal number of children in mind. And they are among the most likely to value traditional gender and family arrangements.[6] The flipside of that is they tend to be among the least likely to be completely childless or to think childlessness is ideal, for them personally or for society. And for the evangelical families I interviewed, even in the face of insurmountable infertility, the idea of accepting childlessness was unthinkable—maybe even sinful.[7] Adoption was really the only acceptable option left.

Why didn't all these families just say that? And why didn't all the journalists ask? The discrepancy in accounts points to a foundational Anglo-Protestant assumption. It's an assumption that extends far beyond just these evangelical communities, which is why secular journalists were so quick to buy the testimonials of these adoptive families as statements of fact. This is the assumption that religious action is driven by faith in some theological idea. On the contrary, as is more the rule than the exception, theology came later.

Occasionally leaders would even acknowledge this fact. Dan Cruver, who was among the leaders promoting the "theology of adoption," confessed, "It has been my experience that many people do not begin thinking about Adoption theologically until they themselves are involved in adopting (or at least considering adopting) a child. Very often, the consideration to adopt a child precedes the consideration of the truth that God has graciously adopted us to be His children."[8] This was precisely my observation. For most families, it was only *after* they started down the path of adoption, when they started reading books, attending conferences, and talking to adoptive families, that they began to learn and reproduce the theological language to narrate their own journey to themselves and others.

This is where the dominant Anglo-Protestant understanding of religion—and white evangelicalism is perhaps the purest example of this—effectively made it more difficult for insiders and outsiders alike to discern what was really going on. The problem wasn't that community norms and social identity concerns were driving Christian couples' desire for children in the face of infertility. But there was a clear expectation that their motives *had* to be articulated in faith-centric terms when the context made their Christian identities salient. Like Brian and Lauren Davis in our interview, when talking to a sociologist about their life history, their reporting was less adorned with theological language and spiritual significance. The context didn't call for it. But when relaying their story to a Christian audience in the video or to other Christians on a fundraising website, they articulated their story in terms their community would expect: faith in theological truth drove their decision. They employed what sociologist C. Wright Mills called "vocabularies of motive." Not lies. And not "bullshit" in the sense that Harry Frankfurt describes as a sort of impression management that hinges on deliberate misrepresentation. But these were reinterpreted accounts of their actions retrofitted to community expectations by people who share those same expectations. Their account was how things *should* go according to their own understanding of how religion works.[9]

Sociologists have for decades observed this same pattern in the stories we tell about our own religious conversions. In learning how to *be* a good [Muslim, Mormon, Catholic, etc.], not only must new converts learn a new set of norms, formal rituals, and theological outlooks but also their religious education often includes learning how to reinterpret their own life in religious terms and to retell their story in community-approved ways. The content and even structure of their narratives end up sounding strangely similar. What more often unfolds as a highly idiosyncratic process of exchanging old relationships and social identities for new ones becomes a miraculous story of one miserable and wretched sinner's near-instantaneous transformation at realizing "the truth" (I once was blind, but now I see). So it was the case in evangelicals' adoption accounts.[10]

Now imagine the majority of evangelical adoptive and fostering families recounting the same story in conversations, video testimonials, and books. And imagine outsiders inclined to take those accounts at face value. What you get is the impression that hundreds, or even thousands, of Christian families have been swept up in a new theological movement that shows no signs of slowing.

The reality, however, was that most of these families were adopting or fostering for the same reasons such families have always done so: to have children that they couldn't have through more traditional means. This is why the adoption or fostering numbers didn't change. The movement hadn't created new motives for Christians to adopt or foster children. (In fact, we may be observing diminishing motives among Christian families to have children at all.) It had created new "vocabularies of motive" for such families to explain their behavior to each other and the world.

What about evangelical families who already had biological children and adopted later? Certainly, there were those families in my study too. But their stories had common patterns as well. First, many of these families had also been prevented from having as many biological children as they would've wanted, due to pregnancy complications, endometriosis, or genetic concerns. Adoption was still primarily a way to have the family they'd envisioned rather than (at least initially) an act of faithful obedience. But among those families who adopted after they'd had plenty of biological children, there was another pattern. Almost to the person, each one held a central position in their church communities, either as lay elders or pastors. These were not junior varsity evangelicals on the fringes. They were varsity—team captains and coaches, in fact. In other words, these were families whose social identities were characterized by serious Christian living and leadership. And when adoption becomes synonymous with Christian leadership, like leading in church, homeschooling children, publicly advocating for pro-life causes, or voting a certain way, it becomes a norm—a form of identity-in-practice.

As I'll share in chapters ahead, emerging evidence suggests what I found among families involved in the evangelical orphan care movement is a more accurate picture of how religion works in reality. What seems to drive religious behavior, like any other social behavior, is less about theological belief and more about the deep culture of community norms and social identities. Our theological beliefs become a way we orient our behavior according to community expectations, reaffirming "this is who we are" and "this is why we do things." But there's another reason movement leaders and journalists were so easily misled about the Christian orphan care activism. It represents a fundamental misunderstanding of trends in Christian family formation practices and the preeminence of such trends over even the most popular fads in Christian teaching.

Patterns More than Preaching

Few scholars would reduce "religion" to mere faith in ideas. But some have gotten close. In their classic book *Acts of Faith: Explaining the Human Side of Religion*, sociologists Rodney Stark and Roger Finke argue that "Religion is first and foremost an intellectual product, and *ideas* are its truly fundamental aspect."[11] Their view does not represent the consensus in religion scholarship. But it does reflect our dominant Anglo-Protestant culture, which is characterized by a commitment to "idealism." Though scholars can mean different things by the term, I use it in the philosophical sense that "ideas" hold some fundamental reality and primacy. I'll unpack this further in chapters ahead, but the Anglo-Protestant Christian tradition is profoundly idealistic, holding not only that ideas about God and humanity matter but also that they are the primary agents of change. Change peoples' ideas, change the world. This idealistic perspective supports the notion that the behavior of religious groups, on a grand scale, can be explained by the rise, fall, and transformation of dominant ideas.[12]

Ideas *do* matter. But the ideal*ism* of our Anglo-Protestant tradition is often misguided. The powerful ideas that we believe shape the world often owe their dominance less to their foundation in reality, or even their influence over people, than to the circumstances that gave rise to the populations that hold them. The success of our formal religious ideas—the doctrines of our religious traditions—are most often downstream of movements in human populations (demography) and the material-political situations they find themselves in (structure).

The mysterious "failure" of the Christian orphan care movement is a particularly poignant example. Movement insiders and critical outsiders alike weren't just distracted by the uncannily similar narratives of Christian adoptive families. Those narratives were planted in the fertile soil of idealism. The expectation that all the activity to disseminate new ideas to American Christians (the conferences, videos, books, webinars, sermons) *must* generate massive changes in Christian adoption and fostering led to a form of confirmation bias that made the narratives eminently plausible. The fact is, if anyone had bothered to scrutinize broader trends in child-bearing and adoption, or even the prevalence of adoption practice at all, these narratives would've been seen for what they were— remarkable outliers in what have otherwise been consistent trends in Christian family formation that resemble the rest of the West. In fact, we may have gotten the relationship between Christians organizing for adoption and the adoption trends entirely backward. Let me show you what I mean.

Figure 1.1 presents trends in adoption from 1951 to 2022. These trends often strike many as surprising, given the prevalence of celebrities adopting and controversies around the Christian orphan care movement. In reality, non-relative adoption in the sense that we commonly think about it is a fairly modern phenomenon. What is more, it has never been a particularly common practice among *any* population. Even at its height, there have always been less than 100,000 non-relative adoptions annually, and often much less. But the important fact to keep in mind is this: there is no evidence trends in adoption are the result of variations in religious ideas.

In fact, looking at the adoption trends *prior* to the beginnings of the orphan care movement, it could be even more plausible that the Christian orphan care movement was itself a *consequence* of some

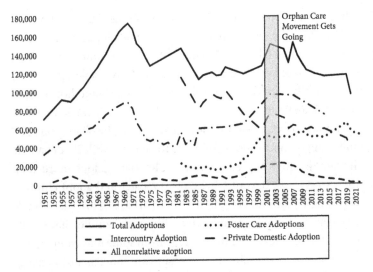

Figure 1.1. Trends in adoption, 1951–2022.
Sources: Johnstone (2022) and author's compilations.

larger surge in adoption interest in the United States. Foster-care, intercountry, and private domestic adoptions were all experiencing a surge in the late-1990s to early-2000s and non-relative adoptions reached an all-time high in 2002. As the gray band in the chart shows, this surge took place right before the movement took off. What started as a small ministry led by adoptive-father Paul Pennington quickly grew to a massive coalition attracting the attention of major players in the evangelical world including James Dobson, Dennis Rainey, Rick Warren, John Piper, and Steven Curtis Chapman. Evangelical trends are often downstream of broader American trends in politics and popular culture.[13] And a swell of interest among Christians to draw attention to the plight of "orphans" and the need to adopt them could have reflected what was already happening on a much larger scale.

But it clearly could not keep that momentum going. Just as the Christian orphan care movement began to pick up steam in the early 2000s, adoption overall began declining. That decline has continued for the past 20 years. International adoption has practically been in free fall since 2004. And foster care adoptions (which are totally free, with thousands of children available right now) have typically varied year-to-year by a few thousand, hovering in the mid-50,000 range in most years for decades. The variations certainly don't reflect a massive movement among the 60 million or so adult evangelicals to adopt children. To be sure, while it's debatable whether theologically conservative Christians adopt more than other Americans, devout Christians do foster and adopt children every single year and the children in their homes are exceedingly fortunate for their love and care.[14] But such families have been around for decades and didn't emerge from some new campaign.

The failure of the Christian orphan care movement to change these adoption trends certainly wasn't for lack of trying. The movement has been going on for 20 years now, hosting an annual conference that numbers in the thousands, promoting "Orphan Sunday" campaigns, publishing books, and cooperating with government agencies. But the numbers just don't seem to change. There is one major "supply-side" reason that I'll explain further below, but we cannot ignore the "demand side" of the equation. One major reason the ideas promoted by the Christian orphan care movement could not change the decline of adoption in the United States is because committed Christians are themselves part of a much broader population trend that reflects a decline in fertility and declining interest in children. Though conservative Christians have historically recorded higher fertility than other Americans, over the past few decades, Americans across religious identity have largely converged in their childbearing patterns.[15]

I'll talk about this more in Chapter 3, but the overriding principle to keep in mind is that religious groups, just like their religious movements, grow and decline largely as a consequence of population dynamics. These dynamics include patterns of family formation and much more. But they are less a reflection of consciously held, rational ideas, and more a consequence of structural factors including political, economic, and technological conditions.[16] That brings us to the "supply-side" issue facing the orphan care movement.

There is something that massively influences trends in adoption and foster care in the United States and around the world—laws and policies. In a word "structures." Look back at Figure 1.1 above. Note the dramatic leap where foster care adoptions more than doubled between 1995 and 2000 from around 22,000 to 50,000. Then they plateau for 15 years. What caused that massive climb? It wasn't a religious movement. There were several changes in public policy that simultaneously increased the number of children in foster care awaiting adoption and sought to more quickly place those children into stable families.

In the mid-1990s, Bill Clinton signed into law the Personal Responsibility and Work Opportunity Reconciliation Act, which changed child welfare policy in ways that put limits on the amount of time parents could receive government assistance and introduced work requirements. Though the reduction in welfare benefits may have been related to rising rates of foster care initially (as parents who could no longer afford their children were at greater risk to have them removed due to negligence), this didn't seem to have lasting effect, as the number of children in foster care peaked in 2000 and dropped through the early 2010s. What may have played an even greater role in the late 1990s was a series of bills designed to move children out of the foster care system sooner. The Interethnic Placement Act (1996) prohibited states or agencies from delaying or denying a child's placement into a family on the basis of race, color, or national origin. This was followed by the Adoption and Safe Families Act (1997), which shortened timelines for birth parents who wished to get their kids out of foster care, lowered the bar for terminating parental rights, and hastened the search for permanent adoptive parents. In short, policy reform, not a shift in ideas, led to a massive jump in children awaiting adoption (because parental rights were more quickly terminated) and in children actually being adopted from foster care.

But we see the same story with international adoption. Figure 1.2 below shows the trends in intercountry adoption into the United States between 1980 and 2021. I've broken this down into selected "sending" nations and regions to highlight a point.[17] Notice the sharp peaks and rapid declines that seem to take place for different regions at different times: Korea in the 1980s, certain Asian regions (Cambodia specifically) in the early 2000s, China and Russia in the mid-2000s, Central America (primarily Guatemala) a few years later, and then Africa (mostly Ethiopia) around 2010. Those peaks and declines reflect a clear boom-bust pattern. First, Americans flock to adopt from various open countries. This then creates perverse incentives to traffic children for Americans who will pay large

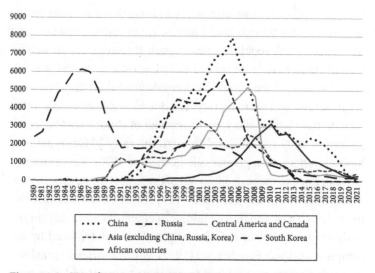

Figure 1.2. Trends in intercountry adoption into the United States, 1980–2021.

Sources: Johnstone (2022) and author's compilations.

sums of money. Then countries quickly shut down their adoption programs leaving Americans to try somewhere else. Were devout Christian adoptive parents part of this story? Absolutely. But they were among the many Americans who were subject to the whims of lawmakers and bureaucrats. The steady decline we have seen since the peak of intercountry adoption in 2004 reflects the legal restrictions nations now place on intercountry adoption into the United States. And it is effective. In 2019 (before the COVID-19 pandemic), less than 3,000 children were adopted into the United States. Since then, the number is less than 2,000.

Has the orphan care movement simply continued on, oblivious to this reality? No, in fact, they've had to shift their theological emphasis in response to the reality of the situation. As the "supply" and "demand" for adoption domestically and internationally have declined, making adoption less of an option, leaders in the orphan care movement no longer talk about a "theology of adoption" that equates Christians' adoption in Christ with child adoption. The emphasis instead has shifted to what is available—foster care. And this gives rise to other religious interpretations of what love, family, and community look like.[18] These shifts illustrate the fact that religious communities and their behavior *always* exist within a structural context of resources, laws, and institutions. And those structures not only guide or constrain their religious beliefs and identities, but often give rise to them in the first place.

As I'll share in chapters ahead, a society's resources, political arrangements, and economic conditions have a direct effect on the religious character of that society. This is partially due to population dynamics like those I discussed earlier. But this is also because we live in a world over which we have less control than we are comfortable admitting to ourselves. And we use religion more often to orient ourselves individually and collectively within that world, and to explain that world as it is rather than to proactively change it. In this regard, the Christian orphan care movement was no failure.

The Christian Orphan Care Movement as a Religious Success Story

On the day I defended my dissertation, I sat with my committee and explained to them the series of discoveries that I've shared above. Summarizing the findings, I explained, "What started as an investigation into what made this movement so successful became an investigation into what made it such a failure." The Princeton sociologist Robert Wuthnow, who'd graciously agreed to serve on my committee, stopped me for a moment and pushed back, "What if the movement wasn't a failure at all?" "What do you mean?" I asked, quite confident I'd shown all the mobilization efforts clearly hadn't budged adoption or foster care numbers. "Well, as a *social* movement it may have been a failure, but maybe that was never the real goal. As a *religious* movement it may have accomplished exactly what was intended. Maybe it became all that religious movements are ever supposed to be."

That question forced me to rethink not only what the Christian orphan care movement was about, but what religion as a social phenomenon is really all about. Like a detective at the end of a murder mystery, swirling details from years of reading and interviewing suddenly coalesced into patterns, and a story emerged that was so clear I marveled how I hadn't seen it sooner.

I recalled all the times I'd heard leaders and authors claim "Christians are too often known for what they're against; but the world doesn't know what we're for." All the times I'd heard leaders quote James 1:27 to other Christians, that "Religion that God our Father accepts as pure and faultless is this: to look after orphans and widows in their distress and to keep oneself from being polluted by the world." All the reconstructed narratives about the gospel awakening Christians to adoption and foster care. All the T-shirts, the books, the conferences, the Orphan Sunday campaigns. I remembered chatting with the movement's founders, Paul and Robin Pennington, in their Austin home. They both expressed concern that adoption (especially transracial adoption) had become a status symbol within evangelicalism. "[T]here's always something new and cool in the church," Paul explained. "When we were younger, it was making bread, wearing jumpers, homeschooling. Things like that." Robin jumped in, "Yeah, kind of a litmus test for how serious you were at that time. . . . But I'm afraid that adoption has become the new litmus test for Christians and especially, you know, in the twenty- and thirty-year-old range."

Maybe Paul and Robin's observation about common patterns within evangelicalism reveals something more fundamental about the groupish nature of religion itself. Maybe the orphan care movement was never really about adoption at all, or even children. What if the movement was about clarifying "who we Christians are" and "what we Christians value" for themselves and the world? And what if individual participation in that movement was more about identification with, and even status among, *our* people?

I remembered speaking with Austin pastor Jason Kovacs. He was one of the leading proponents of the "adoption theology" that connected Christians' spiritual adoption with the need to adopt actual children. He recounted to me where that theology came from. He explained "[The early movement was] very practical focused, very much, you know, best practices. . . . So we said, 'Well, now what would it look like if we just explicitly laid this foundation of the gospel underneath this movement? And we really felt like that was going to be critical if this movement was to sustain. *It needed to be not driven by a passion to help children. It needed to be a spirit-driven passion that was rooted in our understanding of God's great plan of adoption*" (emphasis mine). Did you catch that? Pastors and authors like Kovacs and others looked at what was initially a more practical effort to help children and *added the theology* on the back end for the purpose of making it a more permanent part of conservative Christian living. To create what they called a "culture of adoption" in the church, they believed, required changing the internal and external perception of what Christianity is all about.

They needed to connect helping children with cherished evangelical concepts and the "proper" motives for doing anything.

How do we know they succeeded? Not because of the actual social change, but because of how evangelical Christians became perceived. There was a reason Christian adoption became such a hot issue in the late 2000s. Whether conservative Christian couples were *actually* adopting any more children post-2005 than they had before (and evidence indicates they almost certainly were not), both sympathetic insiders and critical outsiders were absolutely convinced they were. And whether or not their motives to adopt really started with their conviction about The Great Commission and their own spiritual adoption in Christ, that was certainly the narrative adoptive families and credulous journalists enthusiastically repeated. Hell, the narrative was so dominant I dove into my dissertation research without even questioning it!

The movement, in other words, *did change* what evangelicals were known for, both inside and outside their community. Our dominant Anglo-Protestant conceptions of how religion works (faith in ideas driving individual agency) set the expectations. From there, the confirmation bias that comes from journalistic accounts and seeing a handful of transracially adoptive families in your church combined with the consistent narratives of faith-driven adoptions. This mixture allowed evangelicals to think differently about their own faith within a broader context that increasingly stigmatizes evangelicals as anti-everything: anti-abortion, anti-LGBT, anti-immigrant. "What does it mean to be a 'good Christian'? And how do I show that I am one?" Conservative Christians could point one another and outsiders to the orphan care movement and confidently reply: "It means being like us, being for sacrificial love, for children, for the vulnerable."

This may seem hollow, given the absence of practical change, but not if religion is really more about sacralized group identity and norms rather than faith-driven behavior founded on propositional claims. Social movements aim to change the world. Religious movements aim to change the group and its status within the world.

I need to elaborate on these ideas. The Christian orphan care movement provides an important case to illustrate how deeply we often misunderstand how religion works, but there is so much more to clarify about how social identity and norms, population dynamics, and social structure shape our religious futures. In the following three chapters, I'll highlight the social scientific research (including some of my own) that unpacks how religion works in real life. And we begin with the shift from thinking about faith to identity.

2

Belongers before Believers

Group Identity and Norms

In the summer of 1998, going into my freshman year of college, I unknowingly took part in a large natural experiment. I went down to Daytona Beach, Florida, to participate in a Christian summer camp for college students called a Summer Beach Project (SBP). The SBP had been taking place every summer in that city for over a decade. For 10 weeks, students would live in a hotel on the beach, work full-time jobs at local hotels and restaurants, and in the evening ministry staff would teach students how to study the Bible and live as hardcore evangelicals (though we would've just called ourselves "real Christians"). It wasn't all training. Beach volleyball and laughing with roommates typically filled my afternoons, and the social times were spent ritually performing every purity culture cliche: side hugs, girls in one-piece bathing suits, guys swimming in T-shirts, group dates, guarding hearts, confessing lust daily, all of it.

And believe it or not, students came in droves. Several years before I attended, participation in the SBP had swelled to well over 200 students, all from colleges and universities in Georgia. Finding hotels big enough to accommodate all those students became a logistical nightmare. So the SBP directors at some point divided the participants equally into a North Project and South Project based on arbitrary groupings of where one's college happened to be.

Let me repeat that last detail because it's what made the SBP a natural experiment. Whether you ended up on the North Project or South Project was really just about how they divided up the colleges that year, almost completely random. But even though assignment

Religion for Realists. Samuel L. Perry, Oxford University Press. © Oxford University Press 2024.
DOI: 10.1093/oso/9780197672549.003.0003

to North Project or South Project was totally arbitrary, and all these students had come down to Daytona Beach for the exact same reasons, by the time I attended the SBP in 1998, interproject competition and prejudices were virtually an institution, effectively shaping how we experienced our own faith in relation to "others."

I was placed on the South Project. And I had no idea a North Project even existed until that first week when my student counselor—literally 2 years older than I was—told me "There are two SBPs down here. We're South Project, and there's a North Project. They've got a bad reputation for being kinda jerks to us." He also said we regularly conducted prank wars on one another. Fresh out of high school, I thought that sounded hilarious and dove in with gusto. The guys in my room worked at a McDonalds on Daytona Beach's famous A1A strip that summer. All the sandwiches came through me. And whenever I was told that someone from the North Project ordered a burger, I would dump copious amounts of black pepper into the sandwich. Nothing gross or unsanitary, but definitely mean-spirited. And they reciprocated with their own pranks like stealing a banner from our hotel lobby or some other desecration of our sacred honor. At its worst, the animosity between North and South Projects erupted into a full-blown wrestlefest on our hotel lawn that nearly became a violent brawl.

If the situation sounds like it's straight out of some psychology textbook, it should. Social psychologists in the 1970s like Henri Tajfel and John Turner created similar situations to conduct some of the most famous experiments in history. They wanted to demonstrate that human beings can be thrown into groups based on completely arbitrary criteria and almost immediately some human tendency—what psychologist Jonathan Haidt calls the "hive switch"—would be activated. Study participants would favor their own group, assume the best about in-group members, and treat them as individuals. In contrast, the same participants would be suspicious toward their competition, foster prejudice, and treat any out-group members as representatives of the collective.[1]

But what made my experience unique compared to those earlier studies was how those arbitrary identities shaped our religious interpretations and experiences. As the intense feelings of prejudice and hostility between North and South Projects escalated, our leaders decided we should mend the rift by coming together for some joint-project sessions. We would sing worship songs together, perform skits for one another, and hear messages from staff at either project. That should do the trick, right? After all, we were all part of the same college ministry. We all believe the exact same things. And we all came down to Daytona Beach for the same purpose, to become more like Jesus. And literally the only difference between us was the arbitrary selection that put some of us on the North Project and others on the South Project.

But by this time, our competing South Project and North Project identities had shaped our understanding of what *real* Christians look like. They look like us, with all our shared experiences, stories, and warm feelings, not those degenerates. I couldn't help seeing their religious expression through our distinct social identities as North-siders and South-siders. When *our* team got to lead worship, I was convinced our worship leaders were so sincere and talented. You could really feel their love for Jesus. *Their* worship leaders seemed so fake, and performative, and honestly, kinda pitchy. *Our* skits were hilarious and made really important spiritual points. *Theirs* were both immature and inappropriate. *Our* beloved staff leaders gave talks that were life-changing. I took copious notes. *Their* staff leaders gave talks that I could only describe as incoherent ramblings at best and at worst heretical.

Think about this situation. A sample of evangelical college students participating in a summer camp in order to learn how to be better Christians, virtually assigned at random to two groups of equal size with the exact same resources. But the very fact of being segregated into groups eventually led to intergroup competition, hostility, and to a very real degree became a filter through which these students understood their own religious faith compared to their religious opponents. People in *our* group were godly, sincere, funny, and deep—no doubt, true believers. People in *their* group were insincere jerks, immature Christians at best, possibly even fake Christians. ("We don't know their hearts.")

If religion is really about shared faith, if belief is what shapes religious perception and behavior, there really shouldn't have been any conflict. There's no question we all held the same beliefs. And not just about religion, but about everything (culture, social relationships, politics, etc.). But religion isn't fundamentally about faith, or even the content of one's faith. At the level of cognitive and emotional processes, it's about our relationships to in-group and out-group members. Religion is sacralized "us-ness." It orients us within our in-group and it clothes "our people" and "how we do things" with transcendence and eternal, cosmic significance. All the unique things about our religion, the doctrines we collectively affirm, the rituals we collectively practice, and the boundaries we draw, serve to establish us as group members with status just as they distinguish us from out-group members. But it is our fundamental human tendency to orient ourselves within in-groups and out-groups that give birth to myth, ritual, and yes, theology.

Why is this important? Centering social identities in our understanding of religion doesn't just correct our Anglo-Protestant misconceptions about religion's essential nature. It reveals something more critical for understanding our current social, cultural, and political moment. Our traditional religious identities are becoming less central organizing features of our social worlds, even as all our social identities (and especially religion, race, political party, and ideological identity) are increasingly overlapping. Those overlaps have consequences. Even when the social identities are rather arbitrary, they still function like all social identities, inducing positive feelings toward in-group members and suspicion or hostility toward out-group members. And when those identities overlap more and more, because they exert more power when they are stacked than when they are separate, there is a growing synergy of negative feelings and distrust toward out-groups.[2]

Our dominant Western understanding of "religion" needs to transition away from understanding theological beliefs as the primary drivers of social behavior, but instead as markers and intensifiers of group membership. In the service of social identity, theology mostly gives us the tools to narrate our circumstances to ourselves and others. It allows us to locate ourselves within a collective, while also infusing what might otherwise be secular "us vs. them" conflicts with Ultimate and cosmic significance. Contemporary changes in social identities are transforming how we understand religion's social role. They are also creating a situation in which religious characteristics tell us more about Americans than they ever have in the modern era. The scientific study of religion can help us unpack these trends.

Moral, Belonging Animals

Understanding how religion really works requires us to understand how humans work. And one of the most important insights of the social sciences within my lifetime has been that human brains possess two cognitive subsystems that process information differently. Philosophers and religious teachers have long observed that humans possess modes of thought (emotions and reason, flesh and spirit, heart and head) that can seem at cross-purposes.[3] But modern science has empirically supported this idea. And the implications for how we navigate our world and relationships are tremendous. This phenomenon, often called "dual process cognition," has gone by different metaphors. Some scholars talk about shutter speeds on a camera, others talk about an elephant and rider. But the fact has been elaborated in moral psychology, sociology, neuroscience, and economics. Basically this insight boils down to the observation, now repeatedly confirmed, that humans think "fast and slow," to use Daniel Kahneman's phrase. One thought process is automatic, emotional, unconscious, and based on personality and deep socialization. The other is slower, rational, and deliberative. The first one is the source of our gut reactions and self-serving biases, while the second is behind our conscious, strategic reasoning. Guess which one tends to serve the other.[4]

Psychologist Jonathan Haidt famously compares our automatic, intuitive subsystem to the president of the United States. The controlled, rational subsystem, in contrast, is more like the White House press secretary. You get the picture. The president calls the shots. The White House press secretary just publicly justifies what the president already decided to do. That's a bit of an exaggeration. We can make rational, calculated choices that go against our gut reactions, especially when we work in collaboration with others. (Just like in science, different perspectives and accountability reveal our cognitive biases and prevent us from lying to ourselves.) But normally, we're following our intuitions and emotions while using our rational faculties to figure out how to get what "the president" wants and justify it to the world.[5]

But if our rational faculties tend to serve our automatic, intuitive faculties, whom does the latter serve? Certainly part of the answer is the propagation of our genes through survival and reproduction. But along with that seems to be our fundamentally social nature as human beings. Homo sapiens evolved within groups, we exist *only* within groups, and our brains are fine-tuned for social life, including our tendency to divide our world into those whom we consider part of our social group and those who are outside the group. In fact, it seems one of the reasons for Homo sapiens' success as a species is our unique ability to cooperate with non-relatives by creating myths, stories, symbols, and ceremonies. Our collective rituals often involve coordinated physical activities that not only regulate our emotional well-being but also unite us against actual existential threats like enemies, competition, and the forces of nature. Consequently, our social group identities, and our need to protect those identities, are deeply held, practically to the point of us having little discretionary choice in the matter.

Mounting evidence affirms it is this groupish dynamic of religion that is the source of its benefits for individuals or small groups. Studies that examine why devoutly religious persons are happier and healthier than other Americans find this is primarily due not to the comforting beliefs or optimistic outlook religion provides, or even frequent participation in religious rituals on their own, but the deep social relationships that come with consistent participation in religious communities. So too, political scientists Robert Putnam and David Campbell famously show that religious persons are indeed quite generous and selfless with their time and resources. But this is almost completely due to religion's power to solidify bonds of community rather than anything particular about what people in those communities believe. "It is religious belongingness that matters for neighborliness, not religious believing," they explain.[6]

From a social psychological perspective, our social identities and norms (the "way we do things around here") are what we might call "deep culture," to use sociologist Paul Lichterman's term. Deep culture exists at the level of dispositions that are so intuitive we have a difficult time articulating them. We *feel* social identities when our social groups experience victory, threat, insult, or defeat. But there are other parts of culture—different narratives, scripts, stories, strategies, and symbols—that we might call "thin culture." Their application is more optional. We use these when necessary. Sometimes we find them motivating. Often they're just useful to put into words what we were already feeling, or give us a way to justify our behavior to others in a way that is socially approved. Think back on the evangelical adoptive families in the previous chapter using gospel-centric "vocabularies of motive" to narrate their adoption decision and even reinterpret that decision for themselves.[7]

Social scientific discoveries on the primacy of automatic, identity-based thinking over our controlled, rational explanations requires us to rethink "religion" and how it works. We are belongers before we are believers. We have social brains that automatically direct us toward groupish concerns like inclusion, status, stigma, and unspoken expectations for behavior.[8] This requires us to push back on definitions of "religion" that suppose supernatural "beliefs" are telling humans what is good, true, and valuable, and therefore, consciously guiding their social relationships and decisions. We may be "moral, believing animals," as sociologist Christian Smith argues, but that does not mean religions are *primarily* directed by "beliefs about superempirical realities." Rather, as Christian Smith understands, religions proceed from the reality of our social existence and nature. We are "moral" and "believing" largely because we are fundamentally social animals for whom things like "morals" or "beliefs" serve our subjective attachments to groups. The "thin culture" of consciously held, formal theological beliefs doesn't orient our religious lives as much as the "deep culture" of our identities and norms.[9]

That doesn't mean social scientists themselves have remotely made the transition in their thinking. For years, in fact, scholars have pointed out that American sociologists, political scientists, and psychologists are among the leading culprits propagating Anglo-Protestant misconceptions of religion due to our focus on the West, Protestantism, and "mainstream" religion. This has not coincidentally privileged an Anglo-Protestant perspective over basically every other world religion, including Catholics and Orthodox Christians, who have historically recognized the importance of materials, objects, bodily practices, and sacred spaces.[10]

What do we miss with this understanding? For starters, we find ourselves puzzled and frustrated that religious beliefs and behaviors often don't line up as we would expect them to. Sociologist Mark Chaves called this the "religious congruence fallacy."[11] We see Christians who proclaim a gospel of universal love while worshipping in racially segregated churches. We see lifelong ministers who no longer believe in God. We see self-described agnostics saying prayers with their kids at bedtime. To all this we cry "hypocrisy!" But in fact we've made a fundamental error in assuming theological beliefs determine our religious behaviors when they do not. In reality, our theological "beliefs" (e.g., those creeds we recite on Sunday mornings or fight about on social media) are often more like a junk drawer of sayings, explanations, and interpretive viewpoints that signal our membership in a group to ourselves, and more importantly, to our reference groups. In fact, most other non-Protestant religions and religious people around the world already understand this to be the case. That is, they seem to understand their religion as primarily about community tradition, embodied practices, shared readings, special clothing, holy objects, sacred spaces, and most importantly, who they are to the world, not whether they believe certain doctrines from which their whole lives must logically proceed.

Changing our thinking about religion from centering "beliefs" to social norms and identities delivers an immediate payoff. It not only helps us explain religious incongruence at the individual level but also helps us make sense of how groups with the same religion can behave so differently. For example, why do some Muslim-majority countries severely repress religious apostasy and practice the violent oppression of women, LGBTQ persons, or religious minorities, while other Muslim-majority countries operate more like Western-style liberal democracies? Why do evangelical Protestants tend to behave politically one way, while Black Protestants who are just as devout and often hold essentially the same theological commitments behave very differently? Rather than thinking different patterns of group behavior proceed directly from Islamic or Christian doctrine, it is far more consistent with the evidence to think of each group organizing their social worlds according to a combination of history, material context, and social norms that are often geographically specific. Both Islam and Christianity provide a toolbox of teachings that are quite ready to be selectively applied to each context, as do Hinduism, Judaism, Buddhism, and other religions in their global contexts.

Moreover, centering social identity in our understanding of religion also helps us social scientists better make sense of how malleable and situational theological beliefs end up being. Social philosophers have for centuries remarked that each community's understanding of what "God" is like, including his preferences and prejudices, are suspiciously similar to their own. And studies show much of this is indeed the result of projection.[12] Curious to study this for ourselves, my colleagues and I conducted a survey in which we asked Americans to place Jesus on the left–right ideological spectrum from 1 = "extremely left-wing" to 10 = extremely right-wing." As we expected, we found that the leading predictor of where Christians placed Jesus on the spectrum was their own ideological identity. If Christians identified as liberal, or moderate, or conservative, so was their Jesus. But here is an important detail: it didn't seem to be the case that people were adjusting their own ideological identities to match some stable understanding of Jesus, because we found the correlations were nearly identical if you never went to church or didn't identify as a Christian at all. In other words, we found identical patterns among Americans who wouldn't be motivated to adjust their own political identities to match Jesus's. Christian or not, Jesus just seems to look like us, politically.[13]

In other research, I found young people can change their views about God in response to their own struggles with sexual morality. I used national survey data that tracked young Americans from their teenage years into young adulthood. The data showed that conservative Protestants who watched pornography more frequently in their earlier years were more likely to experience doubts about God a few years later. Why? Though most people live with the incongruence between their theological views and their behaviors, many conservative Christians are often deeply bothered by that inconsistency. So they resolve that contradiction either by changing their sexual behavior (often more easily said than done) or changing their theological beliefs.[14] What the two studies I just described have in common is theological beliefs actually being downstream of social identity. In the first situation, people seem to fit their understanding of what Jesus is like politically to match their own political group identity. In the latter situation, people change their theology to resolve dissonance between their social identity and their sexual behavior.

Let me give you another example from politics. In October 2020, just before the presidential election, psychologist Joshua Grubbs and I asked a national sample of Americans how much they agreed that the president of the United States was appointed by God (Figure 2.1). The religious group most likely to affirm that statement was white evangelical Christians by far at 40%. This should be no surprise, as white evangelicals tend to be theologically conservative, believing God is actively involved in human affairs. And

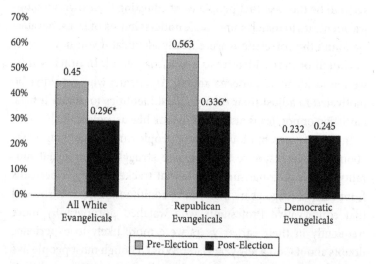

Figure 2.1. Percent of white evangelical Christians who agree that God appoints the President of the United States before and after the 2020 election by party identification.

* Indicates a statistically significant difference between pre-election and postelection outcomes.

Source: Public Discourse and Ethics Surveys, Wave 5 (October 2020) and Wave 7 (February 2021).

they also happen to be overwhelming supporters of then-president Donald Trump. Curious to see how these Americans might change their views after the election, we asked those same Americans the same question again in February 2021, just after Joe Biden's inauguration.

Overall we found the percentage of white evangelicals who agreed that God appointed the president fell by 15% within a span of 5 months. But when we look a little closer at those evangelicals, they didn't all follow the same pattern. Those who identified as Democrats were already less likely than other evangelicals to believe God appoints the president. This is partly because they're slightly less likely than other evangelicals to think God has a special concern for the United States, and also because they didn't identify with Donald Trump or his politics. But after the election, their agreement that God appoints the president didn't go down, but actually increased slightly. What changed? The Democratic candidate—their candidate—was in office. Meanwhile, 56% of white evangelicals who identified as Republicans believed God appointed the president just before the election. But only 34% of those same evangelicals believed that to be the case 5 months later, a 22% drop *among the same people*. The only difference is their candidate lost.

To be sure, Republican white evangelicals even in February 2021 were still more likely than most other Americans to believe God appoints the president. Their theological belief that God is active in the world (even in appointing presidents they don't like) still distinguishes them from other Americans. But clearly their commitment to that theological belief can change quickly when their social group is either benefited or threatened. This tendency for theological beliefs to shift in response to changes in group position shouldn't be surprising to anyone who understands the history of race and religion in the United States. Devout Christians were on both sides of the Civil War and civil rights movement, each justifying either white supremacy or racial equality with their theology. In fact, in one of the most famous books in the sociology of religion, *The Social Sources of Denominationalism*, H. Richard Niebuhr argued in 1929 that religious schisms are primarily about social group concerns like nationality, race, and class; theological disagreements are largely just the pretext.[15]

What Are Religion Questions Really Measuring?

When we understand the fundamental role of social identities and norms in the psychological processes of religion (over something like "beliefs"), it requires that we rethink how we study religion. What exactly are people doing when they answer questions about religion from pollsters and social scientists? Decades ago, scholars began to suspect that Americans say they attend church far more often than they do. And indeed when some sociologists took pains to count how many people were actually in worship on a given Sunday, they found people attended church basically half as often as they reported.[16] In other studies that compare Americans' self-reported frequencies of church attendance to their own day-to-day accounts in time diaries, they also found that people consistently overreport their frequency of worship attendance.

But why do people fib about how often they attend church? It could be related to something we call social desirability bias, in which respondents tend to pick socially approved answers on survey questions in order to make a good impression on some interviewer.[17] But that doesn't help explain most overreporting these days, since most surveys are now conducted online, where there's nobody in person or on the phone to impress. Instead, a better explanation is that survey answers are often better measures of how committed we are to a particular self-concept or social identity. In other words, when we answer general questions about religious behavior or belief, we're first asking ourselves, "What kind of person am I?" and "How would I like to think about myself?"

Think for a moment. Answering a question about church attendance isn't as straightforward as it sounds. How *should* people answer? Yes, they're seeing a question with very clear response patterns. But does life work that way? I personally consider myself and my family pretty regular churchgoers, but this last year we did an abnormal amount of traveling. And the two years before that were disrupted by COVID. Should I factor these disruptions into my average? Am I really a weekly churchgoer? Monthly sounds too hit-or-miss, because I'm certain we've been to church more than 12 times in a given year. So how do I answer? Even as a sociologist determined to give accurate answers to this basic survey question, I'd likely do what most people do. I'd ask myself "What kind of religious person am I?" and, if I'm self-aware enough, "What kind of religious person would I like to think of myself as?" The answer to both is "I'm a pretty regular churchgoer." So I'd likely pick either the "weekly" or "several times a month" option. Are those technically true? Not this year. Maybe not even for the past few years. But ultimately, I'm really answering with my most identity-protective representation of my social identity.

People tend to answer embarrassing questions the same way, just in reverse. For example, in a 2019 survey we asked Americans how much pornography they watched. But we asked it two ways. In one question we asked respondents when was the last time they watched pornography alone and gave them options like "within the past 24 hours," "within the past week," "within the past month," and so on. Then we also asked them to estimate how often they watched pornography alone and gave them options like "once a day or more," "a few times a week," "once a week," and so forth. The first question asks them to report a fact. But the second one asks them about general patterns in their life and consequently gets closer to asking them to think about the kind of person they are (A daily porn user? A several-times-a-week porn user?). These were online and anonymous, so there was no chance of interviewer bias, but the drive to represent oneself positively (even if only to yourself) is still there. And as a result we get different responses in the direction we'd expect. When we ask men about the last time they viewed porn, nearly one quarter (23.7%) said they watched porn "within the past 24 hours." How many men said they watched porn "once a day or more"? About 8%. When we understand that questions are asking about identity, about the kind of people we are, our answers tend to reflect the social expectations we've internalized. Answers about religious commitment, if we'd like to think of ourselves as religious people, work the same way.

This is exactly what sociologist Philip Brenner has documented across multiple nations and multiple religions. Overreporting of religious practices like worship attendance and prayer (and even non-religious practices like voting and exercise) is rampant. And we see examples of religious overreporting across different national contexts and religious traditions. What causes this? Brenner has shown repeatedly that the greater importance someone puts on their religious identity, the more likely they are to overreport their religious activity. In other words, when it's really important to your sense of self to be a faithful Christian, Muslim, or Jew, you answer survey questions to reflect that priority.[18]

There's a similar calculus regarding belief questions, which should cause even greater skepticism toward arguments that Americans' theology consistently explains their behaviors. For example, national surveys often ask a question about how respondents view the Bible. Response options include statements like "The Bible means exactly what it says. It should be interpreted literally, word-for-word, on all subjects." The second most conservative response is "The Bible is perfectly true, but it should not be interpreted literally, word-for-word. We must interpret its meaning." Being raised and formally trained in evangelical spaces, I would wager that the vast majority of conservative, Bible-believing Christians would understand the second option is more consistent with how they actually view the Bible. Very few Christians would insist the Bible must be "interpreted literally, word-for-word, on all subjects." And they certainly wouldn't live that out in practice. But when confronted with a series of options, how do these Christians answer? Understanding that religious persons answer with their social identities, we'd expect that they'd be inclined to say "I see myself as the kind of person who takes the Bible *very* seriously" and then pick whatever answer indicates the most seriousness. That's the literalist answer. And indeed, we find a large proportion of conservative Christians choose that option over the understandably more accurate one about the Bible being perfectly true, but requiring interpretation. And indeed, what we call the "biblical literalism" answer works far better as a predictor of something akin to "fundamentalist identity" or "conservative Christian identity" than as a literal measure of how people actually approach the Bible.[19]

We know through experimental evidence that people tend to approach actually reading the Bible with the same identity-lens. None of us come to our sacred texts as robots processing information. And we couldn't make heads or tails of what we're reading unless we had some sort of background to orient us to what we read. That's usually our group and the anchoring question, "What do people like us think this says?" As anthropologist Brian Malley shows in his book *How the Bible Works*, what people are doing in group Bible studies has little to do with inductive education. People aren't asking "How can I build my theology from the ground up based on what I see here in the text?" Instead it turns out to be more a collective exercise in connecting what they're reading in the text with what their group has already decided the Bible teaches on that topic. He calls this "establishing congruence." Our social group gives us an interpretive tradition such as "The Bible teaches traditional gender roles" or "The Bible teaches racial segregation," or "The Bible teaches that slavery is evil," and we work to establish congruence between our group's traditional interpretation and the actual text.[20]

Putting this theory to the test, my graduate student Elizabeth McElroy and I conducted an experiment in which we had hundreds of students read a famous passage about wives submitting to their husbands in Ephesians chapter 5. But we randomly assigned them to read different Bible translations in which the language of "submission" was hardened, softened, or removed altogether. We found the actual language in the text (unless we completely removed any language about submission and changed it for something else like "commitment") didn't matter much in telling us whether the students thought Paul was teaching misogyny or that wives alone must submit. What mattered even more was whether students identified as "feminist." If they considered themselves feminists, they read misogyny and submission. Conversely, if they considered themselves religiously devout, they saw no misogyny no matter how much the passage stressed "subjection" or "submission." Who we are determines how we read our sacred scriptures more so than the reverse.[21]

But our religious identities have always reflected more than religion. Given that for most of human history religious traditions were geographically isolated, religious identities often overlap considerably with ethnic or even racial identities. I like to illustrate this with my students every semester by having everyone in the classroom first close their eyes. Then I list a series of religious identities: Hindu, Muslim, Buddhist, Southern Baptist, and Atheist. Without exception, students agree that when I said each religious identity they also pictured an ethnicity or race that they associated with it. When I said "Hindu" they thought of someone from India. When I said "Muslim" they thought of someone from a Middle Eastern country. When I said "Buddhist" they thought of someone from perhaps China or Tibet. And when I said "Southern Baptist" or "Atheist" they thought of white Americans. This reflects the human tendency toward association that makes the world easier to navigate without too much thought. But even though it's natural, it's also the basis of stereotypes and prejudice.

This was a key insight of Harvard psychologist Gordon Allport in his famous book *The Nature of Prejudice*. He argued that even though major religions formally teach universal brotherly kindness, the reason they're often associated with prejudice is because religion "usually stands for more than faith" just as my informal experiment with undergraduates shows. As a result, Allport argued, "religious distinctions are made to do double duty."[22] This isn't something we do consciously. Remember we have a tendency toward identity-based, automatic cognition that triggers our emotional responses, gut reactions, and biases. One of the key insights social science has contributed to the study of religion in recent years is that our identities often overlap to where they are *implicitly* associated.

We can see this pretty directly with one of our recent national surveys. In February 2021, we asked Americans how much discrimination various groups would experience in the following year. We asked about groups across racial, religious, sexual, and gender identities, and our respondents could answer from 1 = "None at all" all the way to 4 = "A lot." Here's an interesting pattern: even after I statistically control for a number of religious, political, and sociodemographic characteristics, the leading predictor of whether you think *whites* will experience more discrimination is whether you think that *Christians* will experience more discrimination. But here's the catch, this pattern is particularly true for white Americans. As you can also see in Figure 2.2, the issues of future anti-Christian discrimination and future anti-white discrimination seem wholly unrelated for Black Americans. But if you're a white American, the likelihood that you think whites will soon face "A Lot" of discrimination skyrockets as you think Christians will face discrimination. Why is that the case? Because for many white Americans, being a Christian and being white are overlapping identities. Just as experimental psychologists have repeatedly found that white Americans are more likely to feel "American" implies "white," so too "Christian" likely implies "white." No one is accusing anyone here

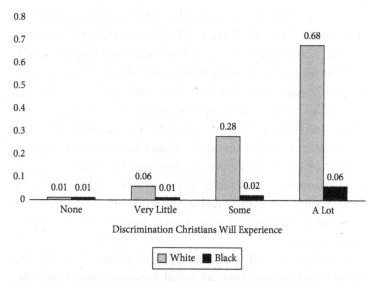

Figure 2.2. Predicted probability of thinking whites will experience "a lot" of discrimination in the next year by how much discrimination they think Christians will experience.

Source: Public Discourse and Ethics Survey, Wave 7 (February 2021). Numbers are from a binary logistic regression model predicting Americans' belief that whites will experience "A lot" of discrimination. Models control for age, gender, education, income, Southern residence, conservative ideological identity, party affiliation, religious affiliation, religiosity, and an index of Christian nationalist ideology.

of being conscious bigots. Would those same white Americans insist explicitly that "white" means "Christian" or vice versa? Almost certainly not. But the connection is implicit.[23]

That last point is important if we're going to understand how religion is involved in our most pressing social, cultural, and political debates. If questions about religious belief or behavior on surveys are better indicators of Americans' commitments to their own religious identities (which always involve in-groups and out-groups) and those religious identities can imply multiple overlapping social identities, what happens when more and more social identities become increasingly aligned?

How Social Identities (Not Theology) Drive
Polarization and Secularization

One of the most notable patterns in American social life over the past five decades is our own political sorting. By "sorting" I mean Americans with particular ideological, religious, racial, regional, and even consumer identities are increasingly coalescing under partisan identities. It may surprise many readers, as it surprises my college students every semester, that in the 1970s, there were roughly equal percentages of white evangelicals among Democrats as there were among Republicans. Two-thirds of white Catholics and the majority of weekly churchgoers identified as Democrats. Neither party was a majority conservative. And as late as the 1990s, former Confederate states weren't all Republican strongholds. Those facts are often surprising because none of that is true now. There are twice as many white evangelicals among Republicans as there are in the Democratic Party. Less than 30% of white Catholics and weekly churchgoers identify as Democrats. Roughly two-thirds of conservatives identify as Republicans with fewer than 10% identifying as Democrats. And former Confederate states are now such strongholds for the Republican Party, Donald Trump didn't even bother campaigning in most of them during his 2020 re-election bid, nor did it cost him in those states.[24]

How have we become so thoroughly sorted? There are a number of mechanisms. One of them is the extreme polarization of our political leaders. Political elites started polarizing in the 1950s and 1960s around issues like race, abortion, homosexuality, and economic policy. As that happened, party platforms and identities began to solidify and Americans across the religious, racial, and ideological categories increasingly learned where they fit. Thus, white conservative Christians learned they're Republicans, secular Americans learned they are Democrats. But this sorting is also caused and amplified by our growing ability to find "our people," both in terms of moving to areas where we're only around people like us, but also through social media and news media.[25]

We can see how these overlapping identities are now assumed among Americans with a survey experiment I conducted along with my graduate students Joshua Davis and Elizabeth McElroy. In spring 2022, we showed hundreds of college students a brief campaign advertisement for a fictional candidate running for the US Senate in Ohio. Students got one of four advertisements that we wrote to be completely identical except for the party identification of the candidate (Republican or Democrat) and whether they used overtly religious language (yes or no). We then asked our participants a series of questions about the candidates, including how religious they thought candidates were.

We found that when both Democratic and Republican candidates used overtly religious language, participants were dead even in how religious they perceived those candidates to be. However, when the candidates said nothing religious in their advertisements, something interesting happened. As Figure 2.3 shows, participants were generally more likely to perceive the Republican candidate as religious, but the difference wasn't statistically significant. But if participants identified as Republicans or Democrats rather than Independents, they were nearly twice as likely to say the irreligious Republican was "somewhat religious" or "very religious." And if that participant self-identified as a Conservative Protestant, nearly three-quarters said the irreligious Republican candidate was religious, but only 31% said the same for the Democratic candidate.

What that shows is Republicans don't have to communicate anything about religion for Americans to see them as religious. It's more of a given. And that implicit association between religion and party identification is especially salient if the American in question is someone already connected to political parties or who themselves is part of a religious community where party identification and religious identification are already strongly overlapping.

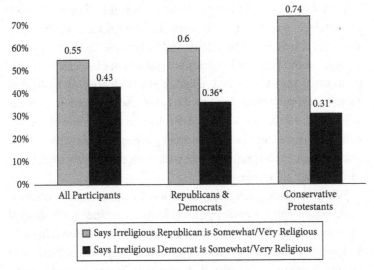

Figure 2.3. Percentage of experiment participants who said a Republican or Democratic political candidate was religious without any evidence.

* Indicates statistically significant differences between views on Republican and Democratic candidates at the .05 level.

Source: Religion in Campaign Advertisements Survey Experiment (October 2022).

So Americans have sorted politically to the point where party, ideological identity, religion, and other characteristics now thoroughly overlap. But I would also argue this political sorting is the result (and ultimately a catalyst) of secularization, from a social identity perspective. Traditionally social scientists have measured secularization by looking at levels of religious practice or the percentage of Americans who hold certain theological beliefs like belief in God or belief in the authority of the Bible. Still others look at changes in the subjective importance of religion to one's life. By all of these indicators, Western societies are secularizing, with the United States lagging but still following the general pattern.[26]

Focusing on social identity allows us to think of secularization in a different way. We've already seen there is a disconnect between theological beliefs and practices. And instead we find self-reported answers about belief or behavior are often better indicators of how committed someone is to a religious social identity. So instead of focusing on such measures to tell us about secularization, perhaps we should shift to think of secularization as the decline of specifically religious identities as the primary organizing identities of our social lives and their replacement with something else—something more ostensibly secular.

What's replacing religious identities? In the American context, the clear answers are more political identities, including ideological identity (conservative or liberal), partisan identity (Republican or Democrat), and as always ethnocultural identity (white, Black, and so on). It is these identities that now organize our social worlds, establishing the boundaries between "us" and "them." The thinking goes, you may identify as a Christian like me, hold theologically views like me, belong to the same denomination as me, and maybe even go to the same church as me. But you're not "my kind of Christian" unless you identify with the partisan, ideological, and ethnocultural concerns of "my kind of people."[27]

This form of secularization combines with political sorting to promote secularization even more. A growing number of studies in political science and sociology, based on data that tracks persons over time, shows our political identities increasingly organize our other social identities, including our religious ones. Those who identify with Republicans and ideological conservatism are more likely to eventually embrace conservative religious identities, while those who identify with Democrats and ideological progressivism are more likely to disaffiliate from religion. And who is particularly likely to identify with Democrats and ideological progressivism? Younger Americans. And some experimental research shows that when young people are exposed to religious or political messages that link religion with conservative politics, if they have any Democratic or left-leaning commitments (as young people often do), they become more likely to disaffiliate. They literally change their religious identification to nothing. And other experiments affirm just the opposite for young Republicans, who become more likely to identify as born-again Christians.[28] This last trend isn't happening enough to offset patterns of disaffiliation and accelerating numbers of younger Americans who are raised without any significant identification with religion. As I'll show in the following chapter, the exponential growth of young seculars has an impact on religion in the broader culture that goes beyond the influence of partisan identity sorting.

But let's consider this last group of Americans who start to identify as born-again evangelicals apparently because of what it means politically. What kinds of conversions are those? Here is another consequence of the broader secularizing trend of political identities becoming our more central identities: when conservative religious identities become synonymous with and subordinate to political identities, the very nature of religious identification changes. Take for example findings from Pew Research Center in 2021. Pew senior analyst Greg Smith looked at survey data between 2015 and 2020 to see whether the percent of white Americans who identified as "evangelical or born-again Christians" increased or decreased during this time. Because of the widespread association of white evangelicals with Donald Trump, many likely would've expected white Americans to run from the evangelical identity like it was radioactive. But he found the percentage of white Americans identifying as evangelical actually increased.

How could we explain that finding? When Greg dug a little deeper into the data, he found that the white Americans who recently changed their identification to evangelical were almost exclusively Trump supporters. In other words, their "conversion" didn't seem to be about a born-again religious experience as we often think of that term. But it was because the white evangelical identity has increasingly come to mean "pro-Christian Trump supporter."

The ostensibly secular political identity is not only driving the religious identity, it has transformed it.[29] It's also transforming how we define what's "religious" and, in the process, helping us better understand how "religion" really works.

What Does It Mean to Be "Religious"?

Remember my experience on the SBP back in college? We on the South Side came to associate our own group with true Christianity. And by virtue of their being the antithesis of our group, the North-Siders became associated with fake Christianity. These associations were so salient that it became difficult for us not to interpret all their religious behavior through their out-group status, and thus, it was inauthentic at best. Now, if you'd pressed us, we would've acknowledged that North-Siders met the standard qualifications as Christians, maybe even devout ones if you didn't look too close. But that's not how we *felt* about them. Yes, they believed exactly what we believed, studied the same Bible within the same theological tradition, and engaged in identical religious practices. But what made us "religious" and them inauthentic was purely our arbitrary in-group and out-group distinctions.

There's something we've misunderstood about how our social identities shape what is "religious." Something that critical religion scholars and sociologists have traditionally argued is the most elemental to religious life. Namely, our definitions of what is "religious" in a positive sense are shaped by our own perceptions of group belonging and loyalty. Scholars who study the evolutionary origins of religion argue that religious practices, rituals, and beliefs serve the ultimate purpose of uniting groups to coordinate and cooperate. As Durkheim argued, religion *involves* beliefs and practices, but it *revolves* around conceptions of what the group considers "sacred." And according to Durkheim, what is ultimately considered sacred is the group itself.[30]

We see this in secular ways as well. Stanford sociologist Robb Willer conducted experiments to understand how activist groups motivate their members to make huge sacrifices. He found in multiple studies that persons who sacrifice more, thereby demonstrating their commitment to the group, move up the status hierarchy.[31] Put simply, we are social beings who are driven by group status, and the currency for status is showing you are ride-or-die committed. Understood from this perspective, what makes someone "religious" as the average person sees it, is likely more about what their statements and actions communicate about their commitment to their own group. Traditional markers of what scholars consider "religious" are themselves incidental and only important to the extent that they communicate commitment.

Let me give you a striking example that not only illustrates the centrality of group identity in defining what is "religious" but also reveals how our more secular social identities like party identification, ideological identity, and race now serve to make that determination. In March 2021, Pew Research Center asked Americans how religious they considered Donald Trump and Joe Biden. According to how scholars of religion traditionally measure religiosity—and how the public normally thinks about the term—this would seem to be a no-brainer. Joe Biden is a long-time outspoken Catholic who has always attended mass regularly and constantly talks about his faith. In fact, leading up to the 2012 presidential election, communications scholars found that Joe Biden referenced religion more than the two Republican candidates, Mitt Romney and Paul Ryan. His religious bona fides were so unassailable, some suggest that Biden was added to the 2008 ticket, in part, as an effort to close the perceived "God-gap" between Republicans and Democrats.[32]

Trump, on the other hand, was infamous for being the opposite kind of candidate we would expect conservative Christians to endorse, in part because of his lack of personal commitment to religion. He openly admitted he had never asked forgiveness for his sins; rarely if ever attended church; and admittedly knows little about the Bible (and often demonstrated that). Then there's the "traditional Christian morality" front, which hardly needs comment for the thrice-married playboy who paid hush-money to pornstars and bragged about grabbing women's genitals. Though he often self-identified as a Christian in front of white evangelical audiences, virtually nothing else in his life would affirm that claim by the standards evangelicals would typically apply to themselves. It should be little surprise then that when Pew asked Americans if they knew Donald Trump's religion, only 33% guessed correctly (Protestant). In contrast, nearly 60% of Americans knew that Joe Biden was a Catholic.[33]

So how did Americans rate the religiousness of Donald Trump and Joe Biden? The majority of Americans rated Biden as more religious than Trump, but there were exceptions, and these exceptions end up being the leading predictors of how Americans rated either president's religiosity. In a phrase, the key factor was "identity congruence," specifically congruence between Americans' political identities and that of the president.

Using the Pew data, I created a measure of how Americans rated Donald Trump's religiosity compared to Joe Biden's. As Figure 2.4. shows, Republicans tended to rate Trump as more religious than Biden. In fact, one's party identification was by far the strongest predictor of how religious Americans thought either president was. And this is after I statistically controlled for ideological conservatism, religious characteristics, and other sociodemographic factors. Moreover, the fact that Republicans say Donald Trump was more religious than Joe Biden is made even more interesting by the fact that Republicans were less likely to correctly identify what Donald Trump's religion was compared to Biden's. In other words, even if they don't know what Donald Trump's religious identity is in a traditional sense, it doesn't matter. The thinking goes: "He's one of us, so he's more religious."

We see the same pattern for ideological identity. The more Americans identify with ideological conservatism, the more likely

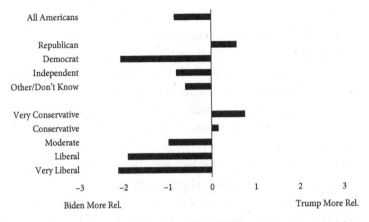

Figure 2.4. Predicted evaluations of Donald Trump and Joe Biden's religiosity by political identity.

Source: Pew Research Center, American Trends Panel Survey, Wave 84 (March 2021). Results from ordinary least squares regression predicting that respondents rated Trump's religiosity higher than Biden's. Models control for age, gender, education, income, Southern residence, conservative ideological identity, party affiliation, religious affiliation, religiosity, and an index of Christian nationalist ideology.

they are to say Donald Trump is more religious than Joe Biden. And again, whether Americans know either leader's religion doesn't seem to matter much. Roughly two-thirds of Americans who identify as "very conservative" know Joe Biden is Catholic, compared to only half who know Donald Trump is Protestant. So what makes either "religious" has less to do with their actual identification with formal religion than whether either is associated with Americans' ideological identities.

But something else also matters surprisingly little: Americans' own religious identities or behaviors. When I examine how someone's religious identity or church attendance corresponds to whether they think Trump or Biden is more religious, neither tells us much. For example, after accounting for other relevant factors with statistical methods, even white evangelicals are more likely to say Joe Biden is more religious than Donald Trump. And at every level of church attendance, Joe Biden comes out on top in religiosity. In other words, what really matters in evaluating Trump or Biden's religiosity is something more fundamental to the core of what "religiosity" means. If we think of being "religious" more in terms of commitment to the group itself, and less in terms of traditional indicators of religiosity (e.g., orthodox theological beliefs, prayer, worship attendance), the connection between political identities and how Americans evaluate politicians' religiosity makes perfect sense.

What about the traditional elements that we tend to think are part of religious practice, like religious gatherings or consistent participation in various rituals? These are not only valuable in binding us to one another, as many scholars have recognized, but vital to the extent that they protect and reproduce our own group identities and values. For their book *Religious Parenting*, sociologists Christian Smith, Bridget Ritz, and Michael Rotolo interviewed hundreds of parents across a variety of religious traditions. They found even the most devout parents prioritized religion's role in preparing their children to navigate life as responsible, moral citizens. Getting their kids to attend Mosque, learn Torah, or get involved in youth group wasn't about preparing kids for the afterlife, or even to be missionaries in this life. It was a way to get their kids around good people and pass along the right values—*our* values. Religious rituals, myths, and social arrangements serve the immediate purpose of marking who *we are* as a people, but also the ultimate purpose of socializing and reproducing *our* people, *our* way of life.

Conclusion

We must transition to emphasize social group identities and norms, as opposed to theological beliefs, as the primary psychological drivers of religious interpretation and expression. The primary reason is that this best reflects the reality of the situation according to mounting evidence. This is "religion for realists." But there are practical reasons why this is so important at the current moment. Authoritarian leaders and their movements understand the power of group dynamics. In particular, they are masters of the same sort of group psychology I've been describing above. They understand what terrifies people, what enrages people, what whips people into frenzies of ecstasy, and most importantly, what motivates and mobilizes people. And they are "realists" about how religion works.

In his landmark book *The Anatomy of Fascism*, historian Robert O. Paxton observes that we can't understand fascism by focusing on the sophisticated ideologies that supposedly drove fascist leaders and mobilized their citizens. Rather, he explains "Fascism was an affair of the gut more than the brain, and the study of the roots of fascism that treats only the thinkers and the writers misses the most powerful impulses of all."[34] Research on political psychology suggests Paxton's point here applies to far more than fascism. In fact, one could substitute "human behavior" for fascism—human behavior is more often an affair of the gut more than the brain. That includes both political and religious behavior. What primarily drives religious behavior is what primarily drives all human social behavior, namely, our emotional impulses, self-serving biases, and unconscious anxieties, all connected to group concerns. And when group identities overlap, as they increasingly are, and our religious identities are increasingly subordinated to partisan, ideological, national, and ethnoracial identities, politicians can actually trigger threats to those primary identities by referencing the religious identity.

Recently my collaborators and I conducted a survey experiment where we randomly assigned hundreds of white Christians to read short paragraphs describing reports of discrimination against white Americans, Black Americans, or Christian Americans. We also randomly assigned some to read no paragraph, which was our control group. We then gave all our participants a survey asking about bias against various groups. Something interesting happened. The group of white Christians who were told about anti-Christian discrimination were not only more likely than the control group to say there was more anti-Christian bias these days but also more likely to say there was more bias against white people. Why? Because the Christian identity implied white racial identity. In another experiment, we found that when we gave white Christians a message from a hypothetical politician about standing against anti-Christian bias, those white Christians also perceived the politician would stand against anti-white bias. For the same reason.[35]

Why are these findings important? Imagine you're an American politician who's looking to leverage ethnonationalist, xenophobic, or racist sentiments to mobilize your base. But you're being watched closely by your opponents and the media. You've got to be subtle. Our results above suggest that religious and racial identities overlap so thoroughly, that you could stoke perceptions of white threat among your predominantly white Christian audience just by consistently referencing threats against Christianity. And you could give leave them with the impression that you'll stand up for white Americans merely by insisting you'll stand up for persecuted Christians. With that possibility in mind, think about the kind of political rhetoric we've heard from politicians on the far-right since 2015. Here are some examples:

> We're under siege. We're losing ground. Christians are losing ground in this country.
> But we're going to protect Christianity. . . . You look at the different [Muslim-majority contexts], and Christianity, it's under siege.
> There is an assault on Christianity. . . . There is an assault on everything we stand for, and we're going to stop the assault.
> You know that Christianity and everything we're talking about today has had a very, very tough time. . . . We're going to bring [Christianity] back because it's a good thing. It's a good thing. They treated you like it was a bad thing, but it's a great thing.

We're stopping cold the attacks on Judeo-Christian values.

Since their loss in 2016, the extreme left has not given up their relentless crusade against Christians and Americans of all faiths.

As soon as I get back in the Oval Office, I'll immediately end the war on Christians. . . . Christians and Americans of faith are being persecuted and government has been weaponized against religion like never before.

In fact, those were all quotes by Donald Trump as a candidate and president from 2016 to 2023.[36] What was he trying to accomplish with those statements? Certainly he was trying to identify himself as the candidate who would defend Christian identity. But given that political sorting ensures his audiences mostly included white, Christian, conservative Americans, his use of seemingly "race neutral" religious rhetoric had racial implications as well. By simply talking about "attacks on Judeo-Christian values," Trump could make his constituents think of Black Lives Matter, wokeness, The 1619 Project, critical race theory, radical Islamic terrorism, and other racialized threats that many also associate with "anti-Christian" threats. And he could present himself as the only candidate to stand against those threats.

Knowing this also helps us make sense of curious events like Trump's famous photo op in front of St. John's Episcopal Church close to the Capitol (Figure 2.5). During the height of George Floyd protests in early June, 2020. Trump had Lafayette Square cleared, walked to the steps of St. John's, and silently held aloft a Christian Bible. During what his followers were told were "racial riots," Trump's declarative statement in posing with a Christian Bible conveyed a message: Trump, the strong defender of Christianity, is also the strong defender of order amid perceived racial chaos. This whole photo op makes much less sense unless Trump (or his advisors) knew his followers would make the implicit connection.[37]

Figure 2.5. Former president Donald Trump holding up a Christian Bible during George Floyd protests, June 1, 2020.
Source: Official White House photo by Shealah Craighead.

We need to understand religion's fundamentally social nature, that even at the cognitive level, religion primarily works through the mechanisms of group status concerns, self-serving biases, and norms, rather than conscious theological beliefs that supposedly transform values and behavior. Otherwise we will not understand how religion is increasingly leveraged by regimes of politicians and pundits who already understand what we fail to grasp.

But of course, there's more to religion. Foundational to the Anglo-Protestant conception of religion as beliefs-driving-behavior is another idea: the *content* of those beliefs are of the utmost importance. It is not only the faith, but the object of faith that makes the difference. In reality, evidence suggests that human societies, and therefore religions, are fundamentally transformed by transitions in human populations before they are transformed by transitions in doctrine. Bodies precede ideas.

3

Evangelism The Old-Fashioned Way

Population Dynamics

Within the first few weeks of my sociology of religion classes, I always pose the same thought experiment to my students: If you were to found your own religion from scratch, and your sole goal was simply to make it grow and overrun your whole society (noble, I know), how would you design it? What sort of ideals would you endorse? How would you train your adherents? How would you position your own group identity vis-à-vis your surrounding society for maximum impact? Remember, it doesn't matter whether your ideals are true or beneficial or your rituals and tactics are ethical. Don't get hung up on the content beyond what you'd need to grow. The only catch is, at least for this part of this thought experiment, societal transformation has to happen from the bottom up. Your dominance must come through people actually *voluntarily* identifying with your group. No forced conversions at gunpoint. No pogroms to take out the competition. No systemic changes to advantage your group (that's for the next chapter). I then ask them to apply their religious growth model to explain the religious data we already have. Does what they propose work in real life?

The conversations are absolutely fascinating. Predictably my more evangelical students will often construct a religion with a message that sounds suspiciously like Christianity, citing an Anglo-Protestant pop culture story of how Christianity grew throughout history. It all started with a small group of followers whose lives had been transformed by Jesus's teaching ministry and resurrection ("the gospel"). Those transformed men shared the gospel message,

Religion for Realists. Samuel L. Perry, Oxford University Press. © Oxford University Press 2024.
DOI: 10.1093/oso/9780197672549.003.0004

which then transformed more lives. Eventually the combination of Christian neighborliness and faithful preaching of the apostolic witness turned the world upside down. Their approach seems to stress the importance of the religious message itself. *Ideas* are key, in other words. Other religions, with other theologies, might not have been so compelling or effective. Those other religions would have to grow by the sword.

This explanation certainly sounds like most evangelical apologetic arguments I've heard for Christianity's centrality to Western civilization and America's prosperity. But it also isn't far off from one provided by none other than the eminent sociologist Christian Smith in the mid-2000s. In his article "Why Christianity Works," published in our flagship *Sociology of Religion* journal, Smith asked readers to consider why Christianity has flourished around the world for two millennia, withstanding persecution and "the acids of modernity." He argued this was because Christianity's theological contents somewhat uniquely meet adherents' emotional needs for security, personal significance, unconditional love, confession, forgiveness, transcendent worship, and community belonging.[1]

But back to class. I then ask my students to unpack why different Christian groups grow and decline. True to form, they fall back on the same story. By that time in the semester, for example, they've learned mainline Protestant denominations in the United States have been declining for decades while evangelical denominations have grown or held steady. Just as I frequently heard in my evangelical churches growing up, the students explain that greater faithfulness to "biblical" teaching produced growth while those liberal mainliners compromised the message and saw the fruits of their waywardness. Again, the ideas are key. Interestingly enough, the premise of this argument is shared by the so-called New Atheists, who see pervasive religious (false) ideas as the world's core problem, and the proliferation of secular (true) ideas as the solution.[2]

But my evangelical students have a difficult time explaining why conservative Protestant denominations like the Southern Baptist

Convention and the Lutheran Missouri Synod, who institutionally are as staunchly true to their message as ever, are also seeing
consistent, measurable declines, while groups like the Jehovah's
Witnesses and Latter Day Saints (at least for now) are showing
growth. And what about the global advance of Islam, growing at
a much faster rate than Christianity or secularism?[3] Is that due to
Islam's superior doctrines and underlying ideas? Should Christian
Smith publish a follow-up article called "Why Islam Works"?

Others in the class focus less on the content of the religious message and more on the energy and organization put toward attracting
new followers. In their religion, they would above all stress the need
to evangelize and train their followers to make disciples, avoiding
all distractions like politics or intentional culture-building. This at
least better explains the smaller sects above. If Latter Day Saints and
Jehovah's Witnesses are growing, they reason, it's probably because
they both work so hard at evangelism, sending out missionaries,
publishing literature, going door-to-door, and convincing people
to convert. They also stay in their lane, eschewing culture-warring
campaigns that may alienate people needlessly (see the previous
chapter). Conversely, if mainline denominations like Methodists
and Episcopalians are in decline, it's probably because they're stuck
in their stuffy churches and don't bother trying to convert others.

This view at least finds some support in the data. According to the
massive Pew Religious Landscape Study done in 2014, roughly 60%
of Latter Day Saints claim to share their religion with "nonbelievers"
at least monthly, and over 75% of Jehovah's Witnesses share their
religion at least weekly! Meanwhile, nearly 60% of Episcopalians
say they "seldom" or "never" share their religious faith with others.
Whether these numbers reflect actual frequencies or, as we saw in
the previous chapter, are best understood as expressions of identity,
we could nevertheless conclude evangelism is a more dominant
norm for some religious groups than for others.[4]

But what about the growth of Islam and secular Americans?
Are they engaged in aggressive proselytizing? Many committed

Christians would say they are. But in fact, that Pew data I cited above shows American Muslims claim to share their faith much less than the average Baptist or Pentecostal Christian. And in every category of secular American (atheist, agnostics, and nones), members share their views on religion even less than the average Episcopalian. So while aggressive evangelism may be a strategy that explains the growth of some smaller Christian sects, it doesn't seem to work that way for American seculars, who are growing faster than any other group in the United States. And it's unlikely to explain the remarkable rise of Islam around the world. Even though Pew data show a high percentage of Muslims in Africa and Asia feel converting others is a religious duty, roughly two-thirds of Muslims in Indonesia (where the largest percentage of the world's Muslims live) disagree with that view. And here's another wrinkle to consider: though the population of secular persons is exploding in the United States as it has in other Western nations, seculars are shrinking as a percentage of the global population—at least for now.

So if we were designing a religion to grow, psychologically compelling ideas and militant evangelistic fervor sound exactly like the strategy we'd expect from a society dominated by Anglo-Protestant conceptions of religion. In fact, much of what we're told about Christian denominational growth and hegemonic dominance in the United States is built on that understanding. The Christian denominations that grew the fastest, the thinking goes, were the ones whose ideas closely aligned with our democratic, populist spirit and whose preachers invented novel ways to convert the masses. But in reality, those factors only get us so far in explaining broader religious trends. Clearly we're missing something.

Then I reveal the point of the exercise by showing my students the Amish, that insular group of Christians concentrated in states like Ohio and Pennsylvania who are famous for avoiding technology and shunning dissenters. Amish communities for the most part hold to orthodox Protestant teachings, but it's not their literalist reading of conservative Protestant doctrines that makes them unique.[5] They're actually an excellent group to highlight the reality I stressed in the previous chapter: theological interpretation is typically downstream of group identity and norms. In the case of the Amish, their uniqueness comes from their "Ordnung" or the unspoken ordinances of their cultural tradition. This shapes their reading of the Bible to stress, for example, the few verses on simplicity and ignore the ones on taking the gospel to all nations. In fact, not only do the Amish avoid direct evangelism. It's almost like they're *trying* to repel new converts. They're famously and intentionally out of step with our technological times. They wear strange clothes and uncool hairstyles. They call their members to a plain, serious life, and they draw a hard line about membership. No halfway. You're in or you're out. By every explanation students give for why religious groups would grow or decline, the Amish should be down to zero by now.

But they're still here—and growing. Figure 3.1 incorporates data from the actual growth of the Amish from 1900 to 2022 and projects their growth to 2055. To be sure, even by 2055, the number of Old-Order Amish is only projected to be around 1 million. They're not taking over the country. But their growth until now has remained steady.

How's that possible? It's possible because the Amish have traditionally averaged well over five children per woman; and roughly 85% of those children will remain in the Amish community, where they will internalize Amish identity and group norms to also have large Amish families (because those who don't internalize those norms are shown the door).[6] More generally, it's possible because their trajectory of religious growth, and possibly their decline in the future, has most consistently been shaped by normal, quite-discernable dynamics of population change.

The social sciences teach us human beings are cognitively fine-tuned for group life, and consequently, group identity and norms, not "beliefs," are the primary cognitive drivers of religious behavior. But a more comprehensive understanding of religious change must

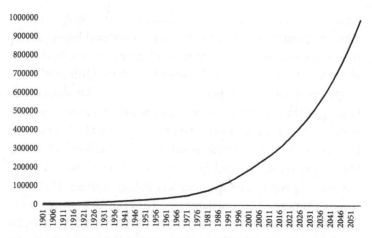

Figure 3.1. Previous and projected growth of old older Amish.

Source: Stone (2017); Amish Studies Center at Elizabethtown College (2023). After 2022, I extrapolate growth using a very conservative estimate of 3% per year, which is quite low (leading to a doubling rate of about 24 years, compared to the rate of about 20 years estimated by Donnermeyer 2015).

take into account what we know about how larger groups in general change: not through the spread of ideas or doctrines primarily, but through the spread of bodies and the durable identities and norms that spread with them. The scientific study of religion is taking what we know about the dynamic relationship between human populations and their social identities and transforming our understanding of our religious future. It's showing us our national and global religious future will look much different in the decades ahead—and it's showing us why.

Debate Competitions, Markets, or Ecologies?

Because the dominant Anglo-Protestant conception of religion is *idealistic*, seeing ideas themselves as critical elements of societal transformation, my students' views about religious growth or decline are entirely expected, which is why I keep running this little thought experiment each year.[7] Students initially expect certain religions or irreligion to flourish on the basis of either religious ideas themselves being inherently better and transformative or the apostles of those ideas being more fervent and organized. Many times, in fact, that's the story we're told about American religion.

What cursory details students get about American religious movements like the First and Second Great Awakenings will tend to emphasize how Jonathan Edwards, George Whitefield, and John Wesley confronted the complacent, watered-down Christianity of the British Colonies with the charge to fully embrace gospel conversion. Or they might include the innovative camp meetings and revival tactics that preachers like Charles Finney devised for converting masses, tactics employed ever since, from the Crusades of Billy Graham to the typical Southern Baptist altar call each Sunday. Or in more sophisticated historical analyses, readers might learn that the religious ideas of movements like the Second Great Awakening (c. 1800–1830 CE) were part of a broader "democratization" of our culture. Fueled by the democratic fervor of the Revolution, Americans rejected Calvinist doctrine, rigid church hierarchies, and the idea of sovereign kings ruling us from a distance, in favor of Arminianism and populism in religion and politics.[8] Naturally, when we think about religious growth and decline, we think about transformative ideas and tactics for disseminating those ideas.

There are academic versions of these thought processes that have fallen on hard times in recent years, and rightfully so. Though it remains pervasive, the philosophical "idealism" that grounds much of the dominant Anglo-Protestant tradition has been relentlessly assaulted by evidence. As much as enlightened, rational thinking has benefited humanity in the past few centuries, society has never functioned like a debate competition, where the best ideas can be presented and ultimately triumph over specious reasoning and sophistry. It is not true that, as Ayn Rand wrote, "Ideas cannot be fought except by means of better ideas."[9] The fact is, the ideas that are most closely aligned with the evidence do not necessarily win the hearts of people and never have. And to insist that "the best ideas eventually win out" is more of a mantra or statement of faith than an appeal to historical fact. As I explained in the previous chapter, mountains of evidence confirm humans are characteristically far more committed to fitting in with, and defending, our groups than holding empirically correct views.[10] But even if we were inclined to pursue the "correct" religious view and could somehow eliminate our own biases from the equation, the ideas preferred by those with numerical and institutional resources would always hold an unfair advantage.

But neither is religious success or decline just about hustle. The academic program most closely aligned with that view is often called the "rational choice" or "religious markets" or "supply-side" theory of religious behavior. According to this perspective, demand for "religious goods" like salvation and answers to the "big questions" is rather constant and uniform across human societies. What differs are the supply and the structure of the religious economy. Religious groups work like firms trying to convince "consumers" that their package of religious goods and services (including everything from the appealing messages to potential romantic partners) are better than the competition. And when these firms compete in religious free markets, as opposed to religious monopolies enforced or subsidized by the state, increased competition means that firms with the most satisfying religious content and effective niche-targeting campaigns score the most converts and resources. Those who act like Blockbuster or General Motors, stubbornly refusing to change with the market, get driven out of business.[11]

Sounds intuitive, right? The language of "firms" and "consumers" and "niche markets" seems to fit so perfectly within the American religious landscape. For decades we've watched the proliferation of big-box megachurches, with their therapeutic messages, irresistible lattes, cushy seats, professional musicians, hip crowds, and rockstar CEO pastors crushing the "mom and pop" churches and taking their members.

But these seductive metaphors are wrong. The better metaphor for religious growth and decline isn't a debate competition, or a marketplace, but an ecology. Each metaphor involves winners and losers. But debate competitions assume consistent rules and neutral judges interested in ideas for their own sake. Markets involve growth in a competitive environment through rational exchanges. In an ecology, you still have the idea of competition, but you win by producing more reproducing bodies. And that is the key to religious success—bodies, and more specifically, bodies of belongers with durable social identities and norms.

Over 20 years ago, sociologists Michael Hout, Andrew Greeley, and Melissa Wilde analyzed decades of survey data to determine why mainline denominations had been in steep decline while conservative Protestant denominations had either maintained or grown. Going by the American folk understanding of religious ideas, or even by the market approach, the obvious answer seemed to be exactly where my students would land: mainline Protestant denominations had either changed the content of the message to where it no longer appealed to the masses and/or they weren't trying to recruit new converts. Meanwhile, conservative Protestants were famously more evangelistic, and their approach, the thinking goes, must have been seeing some success at gaining new converts and getting disaffected mainliners to hop over to evangelical churches. But when Hout and his colleagues looked at the data, they found over three-quarters (76%) of conservative Protestant growth came from the fact that their women started bearing children earlier and had more of them. In addition, there was no change in conversions from mainline to conservative denominations over the decades they observed.[12]

The story of mainline denominational decline in the mid-20th century is less a story of apostasy or religious torpor, and more one of predictable population dynamics associated with socioeconomic status. Episcopalians, Lutherans, Presbyterians, Methodists, both men and women, tend to be white, well educated, and established financially. And over several decades they have done what people with higher socioeconomic status almost always do—focus on education, career, and comfort; delay childbearing; and have fewer babies. Conversely, the story of relative evangelical growth in the latter half of the 20th century isn't necessarily one of superior religious ideas and successful tactics. Rather it was more a story of Southern Baptists, Pentecostals, and other conservative groups who come from lower socioeconomic backgrounds maintaining stronger patriarchal norms, foregoing education, and having bigger families.

It's this same dynamic in reverse that is leading to evangelical declines. As separatist fundamentalists have given way to culture-engaging evangelicals, there are increasingly fewer substantive differences between evangelical Protestants and other Americans in terms of socioeconomic status, cultural consumption, or use of technology.[13] Consequently, the former fertility advantage evangelical Protestants enjoyed over other religious groups has all but vanished. In fact, evidence suggests conservative Protestant denominations are declining in large part due to fertility that is considerably below replacement. (This does not include Pentecostal groups, which are growing due to comparably high fertility, and nondenominational churches which are growing due to switching.[14])

In a study also using data from the General Social Surveys, my colleague Cyrus Schleifer and I documented that, first, American fertility is declining across the board, but childbearing among Americans who identify with more frequent religious practice and theological conservatism is declining slower, resulting in a widening fertility gap. This is again a story of norms, in which those who identify most closely with traditional religious communities are able to maintain a distinctive pronatalist subculture, despite broader trends. Importantly, however, we also found that evangelical fertility has recently been falling faster than all other Americans. And this last pattern is not offset by frequent worship practice or theological conservatism as it is for mainline Protestants or Catholics.[15]

We can see an example of this difference in Figure 3.2 below, which shows the average number of children for American women who are 45 years or older by religious characteristics. Panel A shows Catholic women first. Notice that Catholic women (until the 2015–2018 time frame) from the 1980s onward maintain a fertility differential from non-Catholics and this difference has been consistently large among the most devout Catholic women, even in the 2021 window, where Catholic women who attend mass at least weekly still reported over half a child more during their childbearing years than non-Catholics. But the pattern is quite different for evangelical women in Panel B. Notice that evangelical women in the 1970s and into the mid-1980s average roughly one-third a child more than nonevangelical women, but that gap closes throughout the late-1980s and 1990s to where even frequently attending evangelical women decline in their childbearing in a pattern largely indistinguishable from nonevangelical women until the 2015–2018 window.

Why do the most devoutly committed evangelical women look no different from other evangelicals, unlike what we see for Catholic women? Evangelicals have such strong norms of consistent worship practice and theological conservatism, those norms are essentially a baseline for them. Consequently, whatever small variations we see in either don't influence their fertility rates as they do for other Americans. Though evangelicals may have had more distinctive family patterns as a subculture in decades past, as evangelicals simply became more like other (albeit conservative) Americans on basically every indicator, their fertility has converged with other Americans. We're likely witnessing the same pattern with Latter Day Saints, whose fertility has also declined considerably in recent years despite

Panel A. Catholic Women, Age 45 or Older

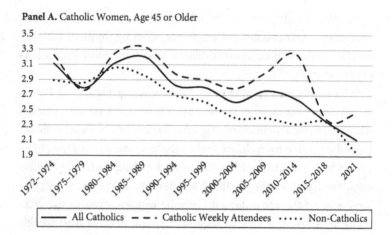

Panel B. Evangelical Women, Age 45 or Older

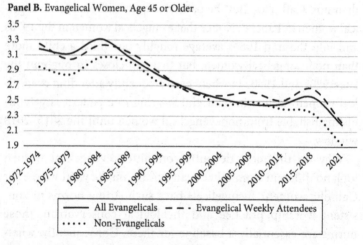

Figure 3.2. Average number of children ever born to women age 45+ by religious characteristics, 1972–2021.
Source: General Social Surveys.

relatively high levels of devotion.[16] The result is that many conservative Protestants are developing a new norm in which their comparably high indicators of religious commitment are uncoupled from high birth rates.

Yet this more conventional dynamic of religious commitment and fertility leads many analysts to predict our global future will be more religious than it is now. In 2015, a team of demographers at Pew Research Center took data from over 2,500 sources to estimate the future size of religious and irreligious populations around the globe. Their analyses of global fertility rates show that between 2010 and 2015, religiously affiliated women averaged about 2.6 children per woman (well above what's called the "replacement fertility rate" of 2.1 children), while unaffiliated women averaged about 1.7 children. Despite the fact that global "switching rates" favor the unaffiliated, and that unaffiliated populations in Europe and North America are expected to climb, the researchers estimated that the religiously unaffiliated would fall from 16.4% of the world's population in 2010 to 13.2% by 2050, while the percentage of affiliated persons would increase from 83.6% of the world's population to 86.8%. These increases will be driven almost entirely by higher birth rates for the religiously affiliated in Asia and Sub-Saharan Africa.[17]

Will these religious trajectories remain steady? I will take up the issue of how broader economic and political transitions shape religion from the top down in the next chapter. But for now it's important to recognize that high levels of religious affiliation and fertility are closely connected to economic and development trends in most nations, including ours. Political scientists Pippa Norris and Ronald Inglehart show that as economic development increases around the world, citizens increase in their "existential security," meaning they don't live in constant fear of famine, disease, war, or political corruption. And when existential security increases, populations simultaneously experience lower birth rates, rising individual-choice norms, and lower levels of religiosity. If that is the case, economic global development would offset the massive religious gains demographers expect in developing nations, contributing to a more secular future.[18]

Immigration patterns are another factor that will inevitably shape religious futures. In the United States the impact can most easily be seen among Catholics. If we were to look at the proportion of Americans who identify as Catholic since the 1950s, we would see very little variation.[19] The percentage has hovered around 25% for roughly 70 years and dipped only recently. But when we look at the percentage of Americans who were raised as Catholics, something doesn't add up. In the 1970s, roughly 84% of those who were raised Catholic still identified as Catholics as adults. But that percentage has declined steadily within the past few decades to where in the 2010s only 65% of those who were raised Catholic still identified that way in adulthood. Figure 3.3 shows what's offsetting the disaffiliation patterns. The percentage of Catholics who are nonwhite, foreign-born, and Hispanic have all increased. The answer, in other words, is immigration, particularly the influx of foreign-born Catholics from the 1990s through past decade. And though that influx seems to have leveled off in the most recent 2022 wave of the General Survey, the proportion of Catholics who are nonwhite, and Hispanic in particular, still climbs. How? This is where fertility differentials come in again, as foreign-born,

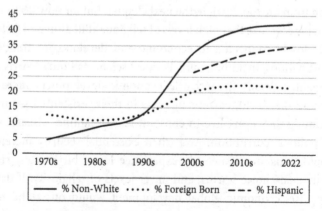

Figure 3.3. Percentage of American Catholics who are non-white, foreign-born, and Hispanic from 1972 to 2022.
Source: General Social Surveys.

Hispanic Catholics have for decades averaged nearly 1 more baby per woman than white Catholics.

In western Europe, the exploding Muslim population represents an even clearer picture of population change via fertility and immigration. In 2010, Pew Research Center estimated that roughly 44 million Muslims were living in Europe, and in the mid-2010s, millions more entered as migrant workers and refugees. Pew also shows the average age of Muslims in Europe is 13 years younger than non-Muslims (indicating more children who will have more children) and that Muslim fertility rates are currently 1 child per woman higher than non-Muslim Europeans. Taking these birthrates and (theoretically) unabated migration into consideration, Pew estimates Muslims could make up 31% of Sweden's population and over 17% of the United Kingdom, France, Germany, Austria, and Norway by 2050. And this growth is projected to happen with a conversion ratio of essentially zero, meaning one convert gained for every Muslim who walks away.[20]

Does religion have anything to do with these patterns? Absolutely. But the immediate point is we're not talking about convincing more people to embrace your religious teachings. We're talking about evangelism the old-fashioned way: either birthing more people who will eventually internalize your religious group identity and norms or shipping in your people who will do the same. Understanding how population dynamics interact with religious identity and norms is essential for helping us understand the most recent religious patterns and their relevance for our social and political future.

But ... Seculars Don't Have More Babies

In the previous chapter, I proposed a way to think about "secularization" that focuses on identity over beliefs. But here it's time to consider how secularization advances or retreats. By a variety of different metrics, we certainly see an overall trend toward secularization in the West, and that includes the United States. But there are a number of theories and broader research programs on offer as to how to best explain the data, with none escaping the odd exceptions to their story. The rise of secular persons in the West, at first blush, appears to be the exception to the population story I'm emphasizing here. Primarily because secular persons tend to have fewer babies than devoutly religious persons, and so one would expect the number of secular persons in the West would decline overall as they fail to replace themselves. Indeed, this is what some demographers and political scientists argue will happen in the future, both in the United States and Europe.[21]

In the meantime, the fact that secular persons are rising in the West at an accelerated rate suggests a larger role for religious "switching" or the changing of religious identities from some religious identification to nothing. This has certainly been taking place in the United States as increasing numbers of Americans who were raised in religious families disaffiliate and remain there over their life course. In fact, Pew Research Center recently presented a thorough report systematically addressing the question of Christianity and secularism's trajectory in the United States. They conclude the rapid changes we see now are primarily due to switching rather than birth rates or immigration.[22]

But population dynamics are more than fertility and immigration. Evidence increasingly suggests the sort of accelerated disaffiliation we are witnessing around the Western world, and currently in the United States, has been made possible by a critical capacity of unaffiliated people. This critical capacity has been produced by a combination of increasingly secular birth cohorts, some within-cohort switching, mixed-religion families, single-parent families, and the asymmetrical retention ratio of secular families. Put simply, population dynamics have contributed to there being enough unaffiliated persons in the population to where secularity is an increasingly live option that people rarely switch back from once they embrace. This then contributes to even more secularity. Rising secularity, in other words, is not necessarily the exception in which (non)religious ideas awaken people to a new (non)religious reality and transform their lives. Irreligious change, like religious change, is preceded and precipitated by the presence of relationships.

When social scientists refer to "cohorts" they're generally talking about groups in a given society that share some experience at the same historical time while growing up, such as children who were raised during the Great Depression, World War II, the sexual revolution, or when the Internet or smartphones were available. Unlike the influences of things like "age" (in which we change simply with maturity, common life events, or nearing the end of our lives) or "period" (in which broader trends affect all of us across age groups), the change that comes from being part of a cohort is different. Here the given situation we're raised in—our experience in society during that time—leaves an indelible mark that shapes the trajectory of our lives. But there is a compounding effect in that persons born within a given cohort go on to raise children, possibly instilling somewhat different identities and norms than previous cohorts might have had. Taken in combination with the natural death of older cohorts, the society becomes increasingly populated with persons whose identities, norms, and ultimately beliefs look very different from previous cohorts. So transformation becomes accelerated.[23]

Among the world's leading experts on secularization, British sociologist David Voas proposed that religious decline across European nations fit a common pattern to where younger cohorts are less religious than the cohorts that preceded them. As this process continues, the socialization processes that would have sustained religious identities and norms (e.g., marrying within the same religion, collective pressure to embrace religious identities to avoid stigma) are eroded and replaced with other secular alternatives and greater openness. In this way, demographic processes of cohort replacement ensure secularization is self-reinforcing in a way that overcomes secular persons' comparatively low fertility. Secular people don't need to have more babies, in other words, if broader modernizing trends, increasing intergroup tolerance, and greater secular competition create a situation in which each cohort of young persons, even in religious homes, has more options.[24]

How does this work? Despite all the theories about religious pluralism and science eroding religious faith by rendering it optional or intellectually problematic, religion has been remarkably resilient. This is, once again, because religion isn't primarily about beliefs or ideas. Rather, religious persons with settled identities and norms who exist within some context where those identities and norms remain prioritized can develop cognitive work-arounds to deal with just about any dissonance.[25] Yet, as pluralism increases, our religious boundaries erode, creating more interreligious marriages and other religiously integrated social contexts like schools, neighborhoods, workplaces, and sports teams. Moreover, as I'll elaborate in the following chapter, scientific, technological, economic, and government-bureaucratic development creates more satisfying secular alternatives to the community resources religious groups traditionally provided (e.g., social interaction, dating options, education, counseling, entertainment, civic involvement). Consequently, each successive cohort of citizens is less socially embedded within religious groups, leading to less emotional attachment, social pressure, ritual practice, and ultimately less attachment to the beliefs of the group. Thus, the secularization process happens through generation replacement and becomes self-reinforcing, accelerating over time.[26]

The broader premises of this argument fit the scientific data. First, sociologists have shown broader cultural changes tend to happen *across* cohorts rather than *within* cohorts. Certainly there are exogenous shocks that more rapidly change society's mores. For example, the civil rights movement rapidly changed white Americans' racial ideology (or at least the extent to which white Americans were comfortable affirming racist statements on surveys). And there's evidence to suggest the rapid acceptance of same-sex marriages has happened too quickly for it to be explained by cohorts alone. Sociologist Stephen Vaisey and his collaborators have studied the issue of cultural change using panel data that follow certain Americans over several years, repeated cross-sectional data to look at broader swaths of time, and even collections of over 10,000 works of literary fiction over centuries. They've determined that citizens don't tend to actively update their social, cultural, and political views in response to new eras or exposure to new information. Instead, they tend to have settled dispositions that shape their outlooks over their life course.[27] Ignoring cohorts, in other words, misleads us about religious change.

Let me give you two examples. Figure 3.4 shows the percentage of Americans who identify as unaffiliated (Panel A) and the percentage of Protestants who specify no denomination (Panel B) across decades and generational cohorts. Note that Americans are generally increasing in their percentage who are "unaffiliated" and Protestants are also increasingly more likely to identify with no denomination in particular. These trends both point to the reality that I discussed in the previous chapter that formal religious identities are growing less important as they get replaced with other identities. But if we just looked at the "period effect," we would miss how these trends are accelerating with more recent cohorts. Notice members of the "Pre-Silent" and "Silent" generations who are unaffiliated or nondenominational Protestants rise only modestly across time. Boomers rise a bit more sharply. Generation X rises more sharply still. And the cohort of Millennials onward climbs the sharpest. This means religious identities are not only losing their importance generally, but this trend is accelerating as the society becomes more populated (and transformed) by persons who are raised in families with less and less attachment to formal religious identities and the group loyalties and norms that accompany them.

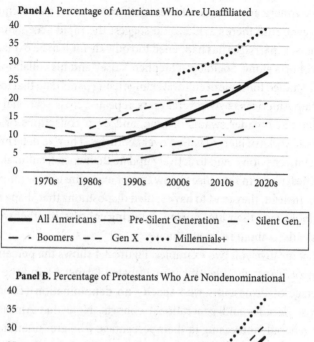

Panel A. Percentage of Americans Who Are Unaffiliated

Panel B. Percentage of Protestants Who Are Nondenominational

Figure 3.4. Percentage of Americans who are religiously unaffiliated and Protestants who are nondenominational across generation and year.

Source: General Social Surveys (1972–2022)

How exactly does this acceleration happen? There are a number of factors at play, and I'll discuss several important ones in the following chapter. But the major factors are also associated with population dynamics. For example, imagine that society becomes filled with persons for whom formal religious identities are either nonexistent or exercise very little influence in persons' social relationships. Then we would expect a rise in interreligious marriages, which would produce more children who may disregard religion altogether or would at least see religion as more optional. And indeed this is exactly what the data show.[28] Moreover, as religious norms about "traditional" nuclear families weaken, so does the likelihood that children are raised in traditional families where married mothers and fathers socialize their children. Indeed, though many pundits on the American right lament that the decline in religious values has led to an erosion of traditional family structure, scholars have pointed out that the association is just as likely cyclical, if not reversed: fewer traditional families means increasingly irreligious cohorts.[29]

Voas's cohort replacement theory of religious decline has since been verified in the European context.[30] But sociologist Simon Brauer has shown the United States fits quite well within the pattern Voas documents in Europe. Voas argued that societies start out dominated by highly "religious" populations in the sense that just about everyone identifies with religion and religion is largely institutionalized and even state-mandated. But as societies modernize, the population of moderately religious persons (those with what Voas calls "fuzzy fidelity") grows as society becomes more pluralistic, free, and open to secular civic options. At first, the population of avowedly secular people in a given society grows slowly because the growing population with "fuzzy fidelity" maintains a social context in which identification with religion is still expected. But over time, moderately religious parents raise successive cohorts who are less and less attached to religion, and these increasingly irreligious cohorts create the society in which future cohorts are born. The avowedly secular population thus grows faster and faster. Brauer shows that the United States is not some strange religious outlier to other nations, but instead is a society that is early in the predictable process of "secular transition," marked by a very large proportion of moderately religious persons who are quickly giving way to a swelling population of secular persons.[31]

And what happens as that population of secular persons increases here? As we would expect from Voas's model, sociologists have also affirmed that secularization increases in the United States especially within areas where secular Americans already exist in sufficient numbers. Sociologists Dingeman Wiertz and Chaeyoon Lim examined the growth of religiously unaffiliated Americans from the early 1970s onward. They found that the number of religious "nones" rose more sharply in states that already had more unaffiliated persons. Is that due to the influence of secular persons? Not necessarily. In an analysis that was even more fine-grained, sociologist Daniel Olson and his coauthors found that American counties with greater religious pluralism showed later declines in county-level religious participation over multiple decades. In other words, rising secularization isn't solely the result of secular persons filling society so much as the normalization of persons who do not share the dominant religious tradition. This fact implicates not only cohort replacement but immigration as well.[32]

A growing population of secular persons, along with increasing religious pluralism, doesn't proactively have to convince people of anything. Part of the rapid switching we see is no doubt due to the fact that persons who were already rather secular in their thinking, but maintaining religious identity and practice because of social pressure, are taking the opportunity to be truer to who they are. Moderate religious affiliation and participation have been in decline.[33] Psychologists Will Gervais and Maxine Najle suspected the percentage of self-identified atheists in the United States (somewhere between 5% and 11%) was suppressed due to stigma attached to the label. When they employed a more indirect method that allowed people to indicate their belief/disbelief in god without directly outing themselves, they found the number of atheists was likely over 20%. The more secular persons in the population, the less likely younger cohorts would feel social pressure to identify with any religion.[34]

Some religious commentators have put a positive spin on that last development as it suggests the half-hearted or "lukewarm" Christians are leaving. "The church is being purified," they argue. But this also secularizes the broader society. And when the broader social context is filled with more secular people, or simply more religious options than the traditional one, secular identity and norms become a live option that people are more likely to take. Understanding this, some Christian commentators on the far-right, whom I'll share more about in the next chapter, are strongly endorsing a return to "cultural Christianity." Though it may have been filled with nominal Christians, their presence more effectively shaped the social context for the maintenance of Christian identity and norms.[35]

Conclusion

At the most basic level, religious transformation is not adequately captured by thinking about debating competitions or marketplaces. That is because religion is not primarily about ideas—right or wrong ones. Consequently, religious adherents are not primarily *believers* transmitting ideas like a contagious virus or "cultural meme," as Richard Dawkins describes it.[36] They are *belongers* transmitting their durable social identities and norms over generations. And historically they have transformed societies with their sticky social inheritance primarily through the processes by which most human societies have always been transformed. In so doing they dominated the religious ecology. These identities and norms are obviously not genetic. People do switch. And the explosive power of cohort replacement is producing a context throughout the Western world in which disaffiliation is accelerating as secularity becomes normalized. We cannot understand the trajectory of global religious demographics, and their implications for all of us, without understanding the scientific insights of population change.

And understanding is indeed its own reward. But there is already a growing understanding of these dynamics among authoritarian regimes worldwide. Preserving the culture of "the nation" or "the race" has long been an obsession of fascist or otherwise repressive movements worldwide. Consequently, authoritarian leaders from Hitler, Mussolini, and Ceausescu to modern autocrats like Victor Orban or Vladimir Putin have sought to bolster fertility in their own nation to stave off the inevitable cultural transformation that comes from immigration and preserve the native stock. Often these leaders have mixed talk of "religious heritage" with talk of the master race or pristine national culture they wish to protect from impurity or corruption. We are increasingly seeing this rhetoric on the Christian far-right in the United States as the prospect of declining religious fertility becomes increasingly conflated with various "replacement" theories regarding the white race and Republicans.

Thanks to popular Netflix documentaries, many Americans know about the Quiverfull Movement of the 1990s and 2000s that stressed having as many children as possible. But the teaching that Christians should have more children to win the culture war has become far more mainstream in recent years. One of the most popular evangelical pastor-authors, Kevin DeYoung wrote for The Gospel Coalition website: "Here's a culture war strategy conservative Christians should get behind: have more children and disciple them like crazy. Strongly consider having more children than you think you can handle." Citing fertility declines among the nonreligious, DeYoung concluded, "The future belongs to the fecund. It's time for happy warriors who seek to 'renew the city' and 'win the culture war' by investing in their local church, focusing on the family, and bringing the kingdom to bear on the world, one baby at a time."[37]

Is there something wrong with that charge? Does this imply anything beyond Christians simply transforming society by filling the world with more Christians? To be clear, I'm not at all suggesting having children is bad (I have three) or that Christians wanting large families is bad. Yet we only need to ask ourselves "Who exactly does DeYoung have in mind when he encourages conservative Christians to have more babies?" Black Protestants, for example, are comparatively just as devout as white evangelicals, if not more so. They are also theologically quite conservative and even socially conservative on a variety of issues. But roughly 85% of them reliably vote Democrat. Is Kevin DeYoung instructing Black Protestants to have "more children than you think you can handle"? Or did he really mean white evangelicals who would help deliver political victories? The context of the broader article strongly suggests he meant the latter.

And this line of thought would be consistent with survey data psychologist Joshua Grubbs and I collected in 2023. We asked Americans what they felt were good and bad reasons to have children. As Figure 3.5 shows, as Americans become more likely to affirm statements about Christians gaining dominion over society, they are more likely to affirm that having children because you want to perpetuate your ethnic or racial heritage is a "good" or "very good" reason.

To be clear, this idea of outbreeding the religious or ethnic competition isn't the majority view even among far-right Christians. Nor is it their practice, since we've already seen devout conservative Protestants are declining in their fertility at rates nearly identical to the rest of Americans. But we do see a pattern with wanting one's religion (or perhaps one's ethnoculture more broadly) to dominate society and a concern with fertility rates. For example, in that same survey above, I found that Americans who think Christians should seek dominion over society are also more likely to support the idea

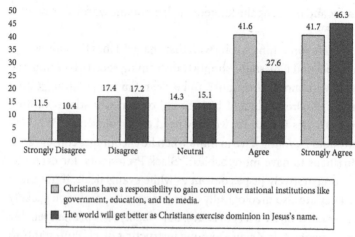

Figure 3.5. Percentage of Americans who believe perpetuating one's ethnic or racial heritage is a "good" or "very good" reason to have children across indicators of support for Christian dominion.
Source: National Addiction and Social Attitudes Survey, Wave 4 (March 2023).

of having children to help reverse the nation's declining birth rates. Are "the nation's" birth rates the same as Christian birth rates? They are if you implicitly (or explicitly) understand Christian and American identities as overlapping.

A more indirect strategy toward bolstering Christian influence in the United States is through a return to patriarchal families, which not only would recenter conservative Anglo-Protestant ethnocultural norms but also inevitably would involve women staying at home and bearing more children. Sometimes this comes in the more benign encouragement for committed Christians to get married and start traditional families earlier. Other times it comes in the form of charges that Christian women have embraced worldly norms such as career aspirations and (in marriage) contraception. In so doing, the accusation goes, such women contribute both to demographic winter as well as normalizing the decoupling of sex from reproduction.[38]

But on the note of totalitarianism, there's another dynamic I've intentionally avoided discussing because it deserves its own chapter. That is the issue of what factors actually govern the changes we see in religious identities and broader population shifts. For what I've just written about Kevin DeYoung's "have more children and disciple them like crazy" strategy, he and the people he's writing to are unlikely to put much of a dent in the religious future of the nation. Social demographer Lyman Stone has shown whatever fertility advantage religious conservatives enjoy over seculars and liberals is unlikely to offset their declining numbers enough to bolster political influence.[39] Yet that doesn't stop leaders like DeYoung from promoting the idea. Why? Because ultimately religious leaders who do understand the power of demography divide into two groups—those who still cling to Anglo-Protestant conceptions of how religion *ought* to move adherents and those who already understand how to more effectively control bodies.

The former (like Dr. DeYoung) still believes they can mobilize Christians in the pews to raise their fertility rates by writing articles, preaching sermons, and driving their bulging minivans around town. Simply put, they still believe directing faith toward the correct ideas will produce the religious effect of more conservative Christian babies. The latter, however, understand what authoritarian leaders have known for decades about directing human behavior toward large scale change—not through sermons, but social structures.[40]

It is here I introduce the other half of my original thought experiment.

4

Come Over Here and Make Me

The Power of Structure

Let's revisit that thought experiment I give to my students about how they'd grow their hypothetical religion to overrun society. You'll recall that I stipulated all religious growth had to come from the bottom up. No forced conversions, no persecuting the competition, no systemic changes to advantage your group. The fact is, I usually don't have to provide that stipulation in class. Most students, coming from an Anglo-Protestant conception of religious life, tend to see religious conversion as personal encounters that lead to individuals putting faith in certain ideas. Thus, they're already thinking in terms of interpersonal persuasion, not coercion. And they rarely know enough about how religion responds to broader structural forces like the economy or politics (at least by that part of the course) to devise a pro-religion systemic arrangement. And perhaps—giving my wonderful students the benefit of the doubt—their thoughts don't naturally gravitate toward tyrannizing their hypothetical religious opponents.

But occasionally I have a bright, Machiavellian, and, dare I say, sociologically-minded student or two who thinks, "Work smarter, not harder." Their reference for growth isn't the early church in the Book of Acts. It's Constantine. They also think about the spread of Islam, growing at least in part by military conquest and imperial governance. They may also think about how the United States was Christianized, yes, in part through awakenings and missionary work, but also because Christian denominations were formally supported by the government. And not just among individual

Religion for Realists. Samuel L. Perry, Oxford University Press. © Oxford University Press 2024.
DOI: 10.1093/oso/9780197672549.003.0005

states. From the colonial era to well into the 20th century, the federal government itself has long shown preferential treatment toward Christianity.[1] Wouldn't it make sense, they reason, to get enough followers in strategic places of influence to start changing laws to support your group? Now we're thinking like sociologists—we're thinking about social structures.

By "social structures" I mean the "rules and resources" that are simultaneously both the consequence of social arrangements and behavior, and the medium through which those arrangements and behaviors are reproduced.[2] Since we don't have a robust inheritance of instincts like other animals, social structures are the ways we humans externalize our norms out into the world so that they organize, constrain, and reproduce our way of life. Put simply: we make social structures, but they also make us, wittingly or unwittingly. The "rules" of social structure include the laws that govern international trade, internalized norms of pick-up basketball, church bylaws, state education policies, and the language system we think with and teach to our children. The "resources" of social structure include the material artifacts and conditions that organize our relationships with one another, our technology, architecture, currency, media, and so on. And all of these structures are related to our religious lives, because religion is fundamentally embodied and social. Once again, we are bodies, then belongers, then believers.

But here's the surprising lesson for my students when we start talking about social structures and religion: there is very little evidence that humans in Western societies, since the advent of modernity, are able to structure their way into making religiosity flourish—at least in the way most mean by flourishing religious life. Societies have certainly tried, but the growing body of scientific evidence suggests broader structural forces, forces that we would not be able to change except by global catastrophe, are further marginalizing religion's historic role in arranging social identities and relationships (see Chapter 2) or determining the behaviors of citizens. Unless, of course, we're talking about a different kind of "religion" than that which we associate with orthodox doctrines, traditional rituals, or spirituality. Another sort of ethnonationalist religion has for the past few decades been on the rise in some countries like Russia. And it may be the religious future of the United States.

This chapter doesn't end with a warning about how authoritarian ethnonationalists will marshal the power of the state to ban science and bring back deeply religious societies. This chapter shows why authoritarian ethnonationalists will try, fail, and create something else completely. It ends with a plea to the secular and deeply religious alike to take a lesson from what the scientific study of religion teaches us about the unexpected dynamic between broader structural forces and "religiosity." Revivals or awakenings of otherworldly religion are unpredictable, and may happen. But when those in power try to revive flagging religious identification or participation in their nation by changing laws to privilege some religion or marginalize another, they end up weakening the spontaneous, personal, spiritual sort of religion further. Or worse, they end up resurrecting, not conventional religiosity, but a Frankenstein's monster of authoritarian ethnonationalism.

Religion against Secular Competition

We've already seen how cohort replacement creates a situation in which Western societies are increasingly composed of cohorts who are less attached to religious identities and behaviors than their parents and grandparents. As a result, secularism accelerates as increasingly irreligious generations make secularity less stigmatized, then normalized, then dominant. But the cohort replacement theory doesn't by itself explain why secular identities seem so much more durable than religious identities in Western societies. Secular people are not near the majority in the United States, for example, but people raised secular are increasingly staying secular, and people raised as Christians are increasingly disaffiliating to "no religion." What is it about our societies that make secular identities and norms, once established, easier to sustain than deeply religious ones?[3]

Scottish sociologist Steve Bruce summarizes the argument of what's called "secularization theory" as simply "modernization creates problems for religion."[4] But what exactly is it about modernization? Earlier social scientists seemed pretty convinced that educational attainment and scientific knowledge would lead to a decline in religion as persons became disabused of "myths" and "delusions."[5] But the evidence supporting this view is rather mixed. On the one hand, studies invariably find a negative correlation, both within and across nations, between educational attainment and religiosity. But it's difficult to determine causal direction here. Are religious people simply less likely to pursue secular education? Or does secular education diminish religiosity? Solving this self-selection problem, studies involving natural experiments show that raising the age of compulsory schooling so that young people were in school longer led to declines in traditional religious belonging, belief, and practice. And others using longitudinal data have shown children raised in religious schools, even after taking into account their religious background and family, were more conventionally religious than their public school counterparts later in life.[6] Secular education may contribute to religious decline, in other words.

But even these studies are difficult to interpret. What exactly is it about the "education" students are exposed to that would lead to religious growth or decline? Is it the factual content itself like math, biology, physics, or insights into human cognition and social organization? Or is it the social pressure, perhaps of one's secular teachers, or peers, or both? Sociologists Miloš Broćić and Andrew Miles used panel data that followed young Americans from their teenage years into their young adulthood. They found that higher education liberalizes moral concerns, but also fosters moral absolutism rather than moral relativism. This was especially true among humanities and social science majors. These findings would suggest higher education, at least in the United States, may include a sort of liberal socialization that is less about the scientific content and more about the formation of secular social identities and norms.[7]

Other studies challenge the typical correlation pattern altogether. For example, several panel studies have found young people who attend college are actually *less* likely to lose their religion than those who do not attend college. And studies have also shown that evangelical Protestants and other theological conservatives do not score lower on tests of scientific knowledge when you remove questions for which they have religious objections (for example, questions about the origins of human beings). This would suggest religious conservatives are often just as knowledgeable about most scientific facts as others, but they simply reject scientific claims that violate teachings at the core of their Christian identity. The issue isn't ignorance or knowledge, in other words, it's social identity concerns. Remember: society doesn't work like a debate competition in which the most coherent arguments or meritorious ideas carry the day. People can hold a remarkable amount of seemingly contradictory ideas in tension for the sake of status and harmony within their group. Consequently, the evidence is far from clear that education, science, and religion are incompatible.[8]

But the oft-observed negative association between education and religion in a society may be pointing us to a more promising structural explanation of religion's decline. It's not that scientific knowledge causes people to disbelieve religion, since theological belief isn't primarily what orients and motivates religious behavior in the first place. But rather modernity has produced evidence-based methods of solving very practical problems that relentlessly fill the world with different structural alternatives to religion. These include technological innovations in agronomy, communications, medicine, and transportation; mental health resources and interventions; recreational and social activities; and government institutions that replace so much of what religious functionaries and institutions historically provided. And societies almost never go backward from these developments, absent some political revolution or catastrophe. Rather, our society builds and depends on them.

Think about the declining influence of clergy in our society. Our pastors are no longer our go-to counselors. We have formally trained therapists and psychiatrists for that. And surveys of clergy suggest even the clergy themselves think that's in their church's best interest.[9] In earlier eras where college degrees (let alone graduate degrees) were quite rare, clergy were among the most educated in the community and thus clergy work used to be a rather admirable profession, one parents would be proud their son pursued. But within the past few years, fewer and fewer Americans say they would recommend their child pursue that line of work, and it has shown the fastest declines in terms of prestige. In fact, while trust in most institutions has declined in the past few decades, trust in religious leaders has declined relatively faster. Indeed, among the growing number of Americans outside Christian communities, trust in leaders of secular institutions has remained relatively steady while trust in clergy has plummeted. The German sociologist Max Weber once observed, "[T]he priest's prestige is in danger of falling with that of their gods." As modernity has reduced our felt need for either, it has reduced our trust in both.[10]

Similarly, the social and civic roles of "the church" have also been replaced. As late as 2000, Gallup showed 70% of Americans were members of a church or synagogue, but by 2023 that percentage had fallen to 45%. And this wasn't just explained by religious disaffiliation. Fewer *affiliated* Americans felt obliged to maintain membership in an increasingly optional social space. Church used to be an important social context for meeting one's future spouse. Now the plurality of American couples meet online. And fewer and fewer Americans want their churches and church leadership to speak into political issues. Instead, Americans look to trusted pundits, journalists, or academics.[11]

Even more than the professional market, however, the most seismic secular replacement comes in the form of the state. Numerous studies, for example, have shown that government spending on various needs that churches or religious families might have historically provided predicts (and most likely leads to) a decline in religiosity. For example, studies have shown that government spending on aid to the poor, the elderly, or education leads to lower levels of religious participation and religious giving in the population.[12] How does that work? There are several mechanisms.

As I mentioned in the previous chapter, research by political scientists Pippa Norris and Ronald Inglehart show that societies with greater existential insecurity (meaning greater anxiety around political corruption, famine, war, pestilence, etc.) are more religious, which they argue is because such citizens subjectively need "the gods" more. But societies with high existential security, where governments are stable and safety nets work, don't produce the sort of desperation needed to sustain high levels of religiosity. Security replaces religiosity. We can see this work in reverse, too, as rapid political or economic transformation can produce greater existential insecurity that promotes religion. Sociologists Chengpang Lee and Myungsahm Suh wanted to explain why South Korea and Taiwan who looked religiously quite similar in the 1950s suddenly diverged between 1960 and 1980 as South Korea exploded with Protestants and Buddhists while Taiwan became comparably irreligious. They show rising inequality in South Korea tracked closely with religious growth as South Koreans' economic fortunes and hopes were frustrated. Rising inequality and dubious social safety nets, Norris and Inglehart argue, explain why the United States has (until recently) maintained such high levels of religiosity despite its massive wealth.[13]

Another mechanism could be that government provisions remove incentives people had for participating in religion socially, and eventually, at all. Economists in particular have been attracted to models of religious participation that consider religious communities as providers of "club goods" in competition with secular providers. People in years past may have leaned on religious communities more for education or help during difficult financial seasons or in old age. And part of the deal in expecting such help was maintaining good standing with faithful participation and financial contributions. In fact, religious communities were incentivized to create strategic stigmas against participating in secular activities or joining with secular organizations in order to ensure commitment and eliminate free-riders. But when the government guarantees education, healthcare, unemployment benefits, and social security, religious communities can no longer make high demands, and participation wanes.[14] And as participation wanes, so does religious giving, which further erodes the ability of religious institutions to compete with the state juggernaut.

But the issue of government spending on education in particular, in addition to replacing the need to stay connected to a religious community, also brings in the issues of competing socialization and cultural pluralism. Instead of religious parents or teachers educating their children within the context of their own particular tradition, students are educated by teachers who generally do not assume the same religious background and, increasingly, alongside students who do not share that background either. The earliest public life of young (even religious) Americans, in other words, becomes a secular, cosmopolitan public life with self-consciously secular curricula.

This happens on a much larger scale than education, as modernization has led to still-rising urbanization, with increasing percentages of our national populations leaving rural areas for larger cities. As the sociologist Emile Durkheim observed over a century ago, and as studies have demonstrated in recent decades, this urbanization results in greater social complexity, cultural pluralism, cosmopolitan social views, and relationships based on market exchanges rather than shared identities or myths about ethnic origins. This leads to lower religious participation at the individual and societal level.[15] Conservative Christian leaders, worried about the encroachments of worldliness, who insist on private school or homeschool and advocate a return to bucolic rural life are not mistaken. If the most important priority is to pass durable religious identities and norms onto one's children—so durable that alternative social identities and norms are unthinkable—years of public education and city life would not be the strategy.

But here is where even the most devoutly religious Americans confront the reality of the secular transition: modernity creates structural arrangements that don't typically reverse except in repressive authoritarian regimes. Western governments now provide social safety nets that religious organizations could not come close to matching. They never have and never could, but even less so as Western societies have grown more secular.[16] A combination of structural transformations and cultural revolution has increased women's opportunities in the workforce and politics. And these advances work in tandem with the state's secularizing influence. Studies show women's suffrage was directly responsible for growing government expenditures on public education during the first half of the 20th century, the same expenditures which other studies show have contributed to long-term declines in religious participation.[17] Moreover, women's advancements in civic and economic life have almost certainly led to a delay in marriage and decline in fertility, just as other Western nations have experienced. But women show no signs of retreating back into the home. And even if they did, the realities of rising housing costs and stagnant incomes have made that reversal ever more impracticable. Public elementary and secondary schools meet the educational needs of 90% of America's children (roughly 50 million in 2023) and that includes nearly 80% of weekly churchgoers.[18] There are no comparable educational institutions that shrinking churches and religious organizations could provide.

There are some voices on the far right who today argue for just such civil rights advances and structural arrangements to be overturned. They are hoping for a religious revival and a return to "traditional" Christian patriarchal norms along with explicit Christian supremacy in American civic life. But research increasingly shows that is no longer an option, and societies that aim for it often end up with something else entirely.

The State Kills Religion, Fast or Slow

Growing up in evangelical spaces I heard a common myth held as a truism about how state persecution actually promoted religious growth, or at least the growth of Christianity. The 2nd-century Christian apologist Tertullian famously told Roman governors to "Do your worst," because "the more you mow us down, the thicker we rise; the Christian blood you spill is like the seed you sow."[19] Evangelical pastors including Billy Graham, John MacArthur, John Piper, David Platt, and countless others have all confidently quoted versions of this idea that Christianity grows when governments try to stop it. It's a claim so bold and counterintuitive it virtually dares social scientists to test it. Is it true? For any religion?

As it turns out, the now-massive amounts of research we have on state involvement and religion, including Christianity, tells us that more government involvement, for or against religion, generally erodes or is unrelated to religiosity and rarely promotes it, at least not in the way most think. Notice I said "religiosity" and not "religion." I mean to stress the common idea of *being* religious as most understand it: *practicing* religious rituals, *believing* supernatural things. State support may, in fact, bolster a resurgence of religious identification, but an identification that is more characterized by nationalist fervor than worship attendance and piety. Let me explain.

Jörg Stolz is a Swiss-German sociologist who has spent much of his career using novel data sources to better understand patterns of religious decline in Europe. In a couple of fascinating studies, Stolz and his colleagues made use of the split between East Germany and West Germany from 1949 to 1989 and their subsequent re-unification as a natural experiment to understand how political and economic pressures shape national religious trajectories. After World War II, France, Britain, and the United States united their occupation zones to create the largely liberal-democratic and free-market Federal Republic of Germany on the western side. Meanwhile, the Soviet Union created a socialist German state on the eastern side, the German Democratic Republic. While West Germany was more pro-Christianity (the Protestant church was even subsidized through taxes), the Soviet-controlled East Germany suppressed religious groups and individuals through the administrative obstruction of worship activities, spreading antireligious propaganda, and applying pressure to disaffiliate and stop religiously socializing one's children. They even prevented children from entering higher education if they did not disaffiliate. These antireligious pressures were at their strongest throughout the 1950s, reduced in the 1960s, and were less important in the 1970s and 1980s.[20]

Were the state's antireligious efforts in East Germany successful? Figures 4.1 and 4.2 tell the story. Rates of disaffiliation, baptism, and confirmation moved in lockstep in provinces of East and West Germany from the early 1900s up until the post–World War II split, which is unsurprising, considering they were part of the same geographically small nation. But Figure 4.1 shows the rate of child baptisms plummeted in East Germany from 85% to 40% between 1950 and 1960, then continued dropping to less than 20% by 1980. Meanwhile the rate of child baptisms in West Germany stayed largely constant at around 90% until 1970. Even after that point, baptism rates declined slowly and never approached the low rates of East Germany in the 1960s.

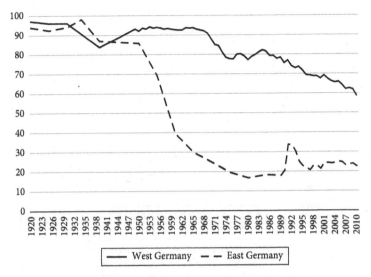

Figure 4.1. Percentage of children baptized in East and West Germany, 1920–2010.

Source: Data provided to the author by Jörg Stolz, cited in Stolz et al. (2020, 2021).

Similarly, Figure 4.2 shows the percentage of East German children who were confirmed in the Lutheran church dropped from nearly 80% in 1958 to less than 25% four years later. These confirmations were replaced by East German parents enrolling their children in the Soviet *Jugendweihe* ("youth consecration"), the secular coming-of-age ceremony in which youth pledged themselves to the "great and noble cause of socialism." Starting in the 1950s, enrollment in this secular confirmation reached roughly 90% of East German children from 1960 to the fall of Communism in 1989. And as we understand from the research on cohort replacement, the fact that the East German regime was able to prevent the religious socialization of children ensured secularization became self-reinforcing.

The result was that by the 1990s onward, the percentage of East Germans who identified as unaffiliated was 74% compared to 23%

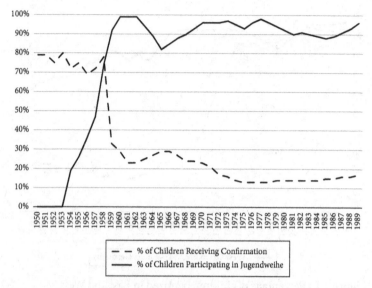

Figure 4.2. Percentage of East German children participating in confirmation or *Jugendweihe*, 1950 to 1989.
Source: Data provided to the author by Jörg Stolz, cited in Stolz et al. (2019, 2020).

of West Germans. But the primary factor wasn't adult disaffiliations. It was having never had a religious background at all. In other analyses, Stolz and his colleagues showed the number of adult disaffiliations in East Germany certainly rose faster than those in West Germany (roughly 10 times faster, in fact). But this only ever amounted to a few percentage points. Yet by the 1990s, roughly 48% of East Germans said they'd never had a religion, compared to only 6% for West Germans. The clear picture Stolz and his coauthors present is that the religious trajectory of West Germany followed the slower "secular transition" identified by David Voas and (in the United States) Simon Brauer, as nations move from religious to "fuzzy fidelity" to secular through twin processes of cohort replacement and modernization. But East Germany followed a completely different path, essentially jumping from religious to secular, largely due to the repressive influence of the state.

Repressive efforts aren't always so successful. China and Soviet Russia, others might object, could present important counterexamples in that the Communist Parties in each historically sought to control, co-opt, and repress Christian growth. In Russia's case, the explicit goal was "scientific atheism." Yet experts claim not only that their efforts were unsuccessful but also that today Christianity in both is growing.[21]

I'll discuss the case of Russia later on. Regarding China, the claims of rapid religious growth are difficult to substantiate because reliable data on China's religious demographics are difficult to come by. For that reason, Pew Research Center could hardly venture a guess about China's religious future in their 2015 study of global religious projections. Other recent studies using individual-level longitudinal data suggest government repression of Christianity is actually quite effective at suppressing religious affiliation and participation.[22] Assuming Christianity is, in fact, growing rapidly in China, analyses suggest it could just as well be attributable to opportune lapses in ideological repression. These lapses open the door for Christianity as an attractive Western alternative to the atheistic, nationalist, and folk religions linked with the oppressive communist regime (more on people making that connection in a moment). In other words, the data are too limited, and the story too complicated for researchers to argue that state repression directly catalyzed Christian growth.[23]

Other analyses have focused on state persecution of Christianity across nations and found essentially no relationship. Missiologist Justin Long cross-referenced international data from Pew Research Center on government and social persecution in particular nations with Operation World's numbers on annual growth of Christian populations in those nations and the combination yielded no discernable pattern. I re-analyze those data in Figure 4.3 focusing on the growth of Christians and nonreligious populations in the roughly 50 Muslim-majority countries in the world. These nations also tend to score the highest on indicators of government religious

Panel A. Christian Population Growth

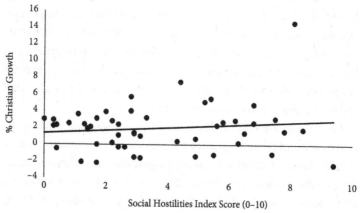

Panel B. Nonreligious Population Growth

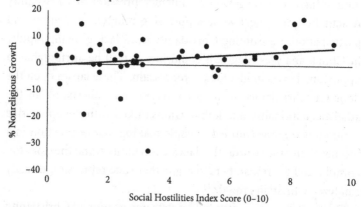

Figure 4.3. The percentage growth of Christian and nonreligious populations in Muslim-majority countries across their score on Social Hostilities Index.

Sources: Operation World, 7th ed. (Mandryk 2010); Pew Research Center, Global Restrictions on Religion Data (2009).

control and persecution. Clearly the scatterplots are messy and the trendlines are so shallow that neither reaches statistical significance by conventional standards. If anything, they suggest a stronger link between religious persecution and people abandoning religion altogether rather than becoming Christians. That is also more consistent with findings I'll share below. Moreover, for Figure 4.3, I focused on Pew's metric called the Social Hostilities Index, which measures the most intense forms of persecution, including intimidation and violence. When I look at their broader measure called the Government Restrictions Index, the associations with Christian growth were even weaker.[24]

In fact, other analyses suggest government regulations *in favor of* Christianity are also unlikely to promote Christian membership or piety. Perhaps even the reverse. In his comprehensive analysis of national religious trends, social demographer Lyman Stone documents how religious disestablishment by various metrics has consistently advanced in the United States since around 1790. Yet his compilation of data also show the period that saw the most consistent drop in laws supporting Christianity, favoring certain Christian groups, or restricting religious expression was also the period in which church membership and attendance rose steadily. Observing the explosion of religious zeal in his own state of Virginia following religious disestablishment, James Madison concluded in 1819, "the number, the industry, and the morality of the Priesthood and the devotion of the people have been manifestly increased by the total separation of the Church from the States." Making similar observations with centuries of church attendance data, sociologists Roger Finke and Rodney Stark famously concluded it was the Christian traditions most privileged by the state that experienced devastating declines in numbers and enthusiasm.[25]

But why would privileging Christianity or any religion lead to its decline in that population? If we citizens make the structures that ultimately make us, wouldn't we expect that human societies who rig all the systems and institutions to privilege one religion are ultimately successful? Not according to the data.

Remember that study of East and West Germany? Jörg Stolz documented that West Germany also experienced its own periodic bursts of disaffiliation. But these weren't connected to persecution, of course, since West Germany actually subsidized the Lutheran church. Instead, these disaffiliations were a response to new taxes that would support that church. Because the compulsory church tax only applied to religious affiliates, from 1970 to 2010, thousands of citizens in West Germany who didn't want to pay new taxes often responded by no longer identifying with the church. Similarly, after reunification in 1990, adult disaffiliation in East Germany skyrocketed more than it ever had under Soviet control. This time it wasn't religious repression, but rather the reintroduction of compulsory church taxes on East Germans who hadn't been involved in religion for years.[26] But this isn't just about nominal Lutherans wanting to avoid taxes. There are two strong reasons we would expect state-supported religion—of the kind that either privileges the majority religion or actively discriminates against minority religions—to lead to a decline in religious vitality.

The first reason has to do with the "supply-side" or "religious markets" perspective I introduced in the previous chapter. While this approach may not have carried the day in predicting the Western world's secular transition, its expectations regarding religious monopolies still prove useful. The idea is that when religions thoroughly dominate a society, clergy's salaries are paid by the state, and competing religions are outlawed, the religion itself suffers as clergy become entitled, unmotivated, and lazy. We may see a direct result of this in studies showing that when religions are more tightly regulated or shown preferential treatment by the government, religious giving and volunteering decline. This could happen, in part, because clergy are simply less motivated or capable of making those sorts of demands.[27] We would also expect minority religious groups to start making gains, since their religious leaders and community members will be sufficiently motivated. Indeed, this seems to be the case. In his 2023 study, for example, political scientist Dan Koev analyzed changes in religious affiliation in 174 nations between 1990 and 2010. He finds that religious groups that received preferential treatment from the government declined while religious minorities gained ground.[28]

The second reason has to do with how citizens think about "religion" when it becomes associated with the state. For one thing, religious regulators are the most likely to become religious persecutors. Though there didn't seem to be much association between Pew's Social Hostilities Index or Government Restrictions Index and Christian growth in Figure 4.3, the two indexes themselves are strongly correlated. Nations with more restrictions on religion are also where we tend to find more violence and intimidation. Unsurprisingly then, studies of multiple countries that take into account a variety of factors show the leading predictor a government will persecute religious minorities is that they exercise strong control over the religious lives of their citizens.[29] That inevitably exacts reputational costs for the majority religion which the government privileges. But even if the government avoids outright persecution—China, for example, scores high on government restrictions, but low in social hostilities—the idea of the government controlling religion could certainly undermine perceptions of religious authenticity. This could help us understand why the more governments get involved in regulating religion *at all* the more likely they are to see religious decline.[30]

And not just in Western or Christian-majority countries either. Political scientist Hannah Ridge analyzed Muslim-majority countries and found that Muslim religious belief and practice were lower in states where Muslims were granted fewer religious freedoms. And focusing on the Islamization efforts in Turkey from 2002 to 2018, economist Murat Çokgezen finds that despite several decades of pro-Islam policies, Turkish Muslims declined in their religious belief, practice, and trust in clergy. He concluded that the symbiotic relationship between the pro-Islamic government and the religious leadership and institutions explain the pattern. Citizens are often critical of their governments, particularly those that seek to exercise undue control over their personal lives. To the extent religion becomes functionally associated with the state, negative feelings toward the state become criticisms toward religion. And this works in reverse, too. In their 2023 study, political scientists Jonathan Fox and Jori Breslawksi analyzed 54 Christian-majority countries from 1990 to 2014 and show confidence in the government is lower in countries where the state props up Christianity.[31]

There is one notable exception to the general finding that state-enforced or regulated religion leads to lower religiosity. Economist Mauricio Drelichman and his coauthors created a data set using information from over 67,000 heresy trials held by the Spanish Inquisition from 1480 to 1820. These trials were conducted by the state to preserve Church purity against the encroachments of heterodox views. The economists then observed how municipalities with a stronger inquisitorial presence differed on a variety of outcomes into the 21st century. They found regions where the Inquisition was more active were slightly more religious over a century later. How much more religious? A one standard deviation increase in Inquisition intensity predicted an increase in church attendance between 1.3% to 3.7%. Was it worth it? In addition to the ignominious legacy of the Spanish Inquisition, we should also consider what else the Inquisition produced in municipalities where it was more active. The researchers demonstrate people in these regions were also more economically disadvantaged, less educated, and were less trusting of people in general. And this would be entirely consistent with decades of data showing regions of the world most characterized by state regulation of religion tend to be those with lower levels of economic development, education, and freedom.[32]

What about Authoritarian States ... Where Religion Is Growing?

Among the few nations that have become more religious in the past few decades, that vast majority are former communist countries. Political scientist Ronald Inglehart and others argue that the collapse of communism left an ideological vacuum that religion—and in particular religions formerly dominant in those countries, like Orthodox Christianity—rushed in to fill. But several of these nations are also characterized by authoritarian religious control, and even persecution.

Russia in particular has seen rapid religious growth since the 1990s. Yet it formally privileges the Orthodox Christian church and is frequently listed by various watchdog organizations among the world's leading violators of religious freedom. Russian President Vladimir Putin has advertised himself as a champion of traditional Christian values. This includes not only promoting Russian Orthodoxy, but also what Inglehart calls "pro-fertility norms" like restrictions on LGBTQ persons and abortion and the official promotion of higher birth rates. Leaders and pundits on the Christian Right in the United States have repeatedly expressed support for Putin's style of leadership (and others like him), citing his strength and advocacy for Christian values. Are these authoritarian nations that seem to have both religious regulation and recent religious growth a model for religious groups worldwide to revive flagging religiosity in their own context?

It may depend on the kind of religion one has in mind. Pew Research Center conducted thousands of surveys with citizens of central and eastern Europe to better understand the resurgence of religious growth, particularly in formerly communist countries. That data show Catholicism in Catholic-majority countries like Poland or Hungary have largely followed the secular transition with diminishing numbers of Catholics since the early 1990s. But some national expressions of Orthodox Christianity have become wedded with nationalism in a way that is largely devoid of religious commitment.[33]

Let's compare the religious characteristics of Orthodox Christians in Russia with Ukraine, a nation also characterized by growing percentages of Orthodox Christians, but greater religious freedom protections. Pew data from a 2016 survey show 71% of Russians and 78% of Ukrainians identified as Orthodox Christians,

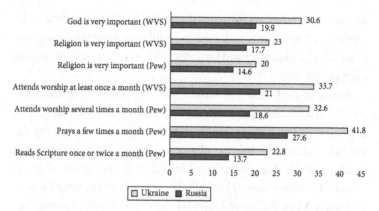

Figure 4.4. Religious commitment of Orthodox Christians in Russia and Ukraine.

Source: Pew Research Center, Eastern Europe Public Data (2015/2016); World Values Survey (2017–2022).

roughly doubling their percentages in 1991. The most recent wave of the World Values Surveys (years 2017 to 2022) report comparable numbers. Neither Russians nor Ukrainians are particularly "religious" in terms of practice, but Ukraine is consistently more so than Russia on virtually every traditional indicator of religious commitment (see Figure 4.4). According to numbers from both Pew and the World Values Survey, Orthodox Christians in Ukraine are significantly more likely to say they attend worship services, pray, or read their sacred Scriptures at least a few times a month, and more likely to say God and religion are very important to them.

But there are some religious indicators for which Orthodox Christians in Russia score higher than their Ukrainian counterparts, and this reflects a broader pattern of ethnocentric, nationalist, and anti-democratic views. Figure 4.5 shows that Russia's Orthodox Christians are considerably more likely to believe government has a responsibility to support the spread of religious values and beliefs in the country, that the national church should receive financial support from the government, and to believe being an Orthodox

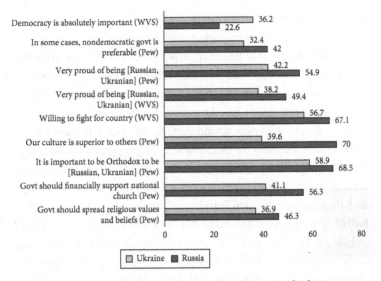

Figure 4.5. Views of Orthodox Christians in Russia and Ukraine on religious nationalism, ethnocentrism, national pride, and democracy.
Source: Pew Research Center, Eastern Europe Public Data (2015/2016); World Values Survey (2017–2022).

Christian is either "somewhat" or "very important" to being truly [Russian, Ukrainian]. They are also more likely to believe their culture is superior to others, to be very proud of being from their country, to be willing to fight for their country, and to say that in some cases nondemocratic governments are preferable to democratic ones. And a question from the World Values Survey shows the flipside of that last belief: Orthodox Christians in Russia are less likely than their Ukrainian counterparts to say democracy is absolutely important.

In addition, Pew data from several surveys show that 85% of Orthodox Christians in Russia believe "A strong Russia is necessary to balance the influence of the West," 72% believe the dissolution of the Soviet Union was a bad thing for their country, and 58% believe that Joseph Stalin's role in history was either "very positive" or "mostly positive."[34] In other words, under Russia's more authoritarian regime and culture, a rise in Orthodox Christianity has not resulted in Russians being more "religious" in the traditional sense. And it certainly hasn't inclined them to link fates with the democratic Christian West. It rather reflects a relatively irreligious, anti-democratic, and frankly rather worrisome ethnonationalism.

Is that attractive for some Americans? It most certainly is. Before 2016, pollsters generally found Americans' views toward Russia were almost identical for both parties, moving only in response to Russia's geopolitical activity. But Donald Trump's warmth toward Russia, his expressed admiration for Vladimir Putin's leadership, and Russia's documented interference in the 2016 election on behalf of Trump caused Americans' views to polarize sharply. Surveys published by Pew and Gallup have shown that not only have Republicans' views toward Russia become more positive but also their favorability of Putin himself also improved, while Democrats have moved in the opposite direction.[35]

But is this just partisanship? In fact, even before the 2016 election, leaders on the Christian Right had already warmed to Putin's defense of traditionalist Christian morality. Franklin Graham, president of the Billy Graham Evangelistic Association, wrote in 2014 that Obama's administration had "turned their backs on God and his standards" regarding same-sex relationships. He applauded Putin's crackdown on gays and lesbians as showing "Putin is right on these issues" and that "Russia's standard is higher than our own." Commentator and former presidential candidate Pat Buchanan also said in 2014, "In the culture war for the future of mankind, Putin is planting Russia's flag firmly on the side of traditional Christianity."

Even after the invasion of Ukraine, a move denounced by leaders in both parties, politicians on the Christian far-right endorsed Putin's leadership. Former GOP Senate candidate for Delaware, Lauren Witzke (herself a catechumen to Russian Orthodoxy) explained, "Russia is a Christian nationalist nation so . . . I actually support Putin's right to protect his people and always put his people first, but also protect their Christian values. I identify more ... with Putin's Christian values than I do with Joe Biden." Other pundits have similarly praised Hungarian Prime Minister Victor Orban, who has likewise wooed the Christian right, endorsing Christian nationalist policies, advocating for Hungarian racial purity, and cracking down on the free press and the LGBTQ community, even as Hungary witnesses uneven religious growth.[36]

But those are pundits and politicians. In a 2023 study, my coauthors and I wanted to understand what it was about Putin that some Americans on the right found attractive. We measured a variety of religious, political, and demographic characteristics, including three different measures of Christian nationalist ideology across three different data sets. We find that even after taking into account Americans' partisan or ideological identification, those who wanted to formally institutionalize America's Christian identity and heritage were not only more supportive of Russia but also more likely to say they admired Putin's leadership qualities. Just as important, we also found that once we took Christian nationalism into account, Americans who scored higher on traditional measures of religiosity (worship attendance, prayer, religious importance) were actually less attracted to Putin's leadership. In other words, what attracts Americans to authoritarian ethnonationalist leaders who enforce traditionalist Christian identity and morals isn't Americans' religious commitment, but their recognition of similar Christian nationalist inclinations in another strongman leader—just as it attracted them to Trump in 2016, 2020, and 2024.[37]

Conclusion

The patterns I've highlighted in this chapter work in concert with the findings on identity, norms, and population from previous chapters. As we've seen, in many Western societies, members of particular religious groups were formerly dominant both in raw numbers and in their cultural and political power. But unlike religious populations in Sub-Saharan Africa and parts of Asia and the Middle East, the raw numbers that buttressed religious influence in North America and Europe are plummeting. And formerly dominant populations of citizens only have a few options when they see their days are numbered, they refuse to change, and they desperately want to cling to power or take back the power that was once theirs. Some seek to leverage the power of identity. They stoke identity-based fear and anger to activate the large number of disengaged citizens who share important aspects of core identity (for example, being Christian and white). Others lean hard into the power of demography. Threatened majorities or former majorities are trying to curb immigration and promote fertility, both of which potentially boost their own waning numbers, or at least slow the bleeding.

But there is a third option. One that often works in tandem with appeals to identity, but doesn't demand them. And this one can actually work in spite of demographic realities. In fact, it's the demographic realities that make this tactic more necessary. This option is to simply rig the system. And if "religion" is primarily about group identity and cherished norms vis-à-vis others, you may not care so much if this tactic empties religion of its transcendent values or personal practices. In fact, we see rigging is a popular choice among those who see their religious past and future as inextricably bound to that of their nation, but see both as threatened.[38]

My goal in writing this book is not to give authoritarian ethnonationalists on the far-right something like a game plan. Rather I believe the scientific study of religion *reveals* their game plan. Thought-leaders on the far-right around the world, it turns out, are better students of how religion actually works because they are less invested in Anglo-Protestant ideals and narratives about personal faith and spiritual realities. They want to know how religion shapes, unites, grows, directs, and mobilizes groups—*their* groups. And as I've shown, the answer is found in the power of social identity and norms, population dynamics, and social structure.

Religion matters now and in the future. And academics like me—those who deal professionally in the discovery and dissemination of facts—have something of a missional obligation to inform the world. But evidence-based religion scholarship isn't handed down like the Ten Commandments to Moses. And it's not disseminated casually or by accident. We need greater recognition in the academic community of religion's importance and the resources (like funding and tenure-track jobs) to facilitate its rigorous study. And to help that research go public, we need researchers, administrators, academic departments, professional organizations, and entire disciplines. In fact, we need whole movements of all these groups who care enough about the humanistic goals of science to earn public trust and translate their work for broader audiences.

In the next two chapters, I tackle the barriers that inhibit "religion for realists." The answer, from one academic speaking to others, is us.

5

More than Benign Disinterest

(Why) Is Religion Research Marginalized?

"Tell me about what you'd like to study," I said to Emily, a prospective graduate student during my office hours. A National Merit Scholar at the University of Oklahoma, where I teach, Emily describes herself as "pretty damn impressive" when she zeroes in on her goals. She's not exaggerating. Graduating early with honors and fresh from crushing the Graduate Record Exam (GRE), Emily is an Oklahoma tornado, ripping through any obstacles in her path. And she's set her sights on a PhD in sociology. I have little hope we can lure her to stay. Like many other talented seniors in our department, Emily seems destined to abscond with her "badassery" (her word) and lofty GRE scores to a higher-ranking program at Bloomington, Chapel Hill, or Palo Alto. During our conversation, Emily describes how her experiences growing up in evangelical churches and her recently coming out as queer shape her areas of interest. "I'd like to study something with gender inequality and religion," she explains. My advice to her is direct: "Let's just say you want to study gender inequality for now. Study religion after you get a job."

That may seem like bizarre advice coming from a sociologist of religion, especially directed toward someone as formidable as Emily. Why wouldn't I push her *toward* religion as an area of interest? Why wouldn't she study whatever she wants? The fact is I may have just saved her career in utero. It's a conversation with which social scientists of religion are all too familiar.[1] There is absolutely no shortage of gifted young people who want to study religion

Religion for Realists. Samuel L. Perry, Oxford University Press. © Oxford University Press 2024.
DOI: 10.1093/oso/9780197672549.003.0006

in psychology, sociology, or political science programs around the country. But not only will they find few mentors to guide them in this effort, the mentors they will find (like me) know part of our job is to help them study religious issues without signaling that religion is their focus. In fact, we actively hide it.

We discourage graduate students from taking comprehensive exams in religion. "Better to comp in stats and some other marketable subfield," I've told half a dozen of my own PhD students. They must avoid religion journals if they can. They must think carefully about how they title their studies, highlighting the key words social scientists find more attractive, minimizing the religion stuff. In their quantitative studies, they must avoid using religion as the outcome variable (unless they're documenting how religion is in decline). Instead they should use religion as one among several predictor variables shaping some other outcome social scientists consider more important. All of this so they can present themselves as scholars of race, gender, class inequality, voting behavior, social identity, or prejudice who also happen to study religion rather than as "religion scholars." And for God's sake, they must scrub their CVs and social media so as to avoid giving the impression that they're one of *those* scholars of religion—the ones who are actually personally religious.

What we're preparing students for is more than just benign disinterest in religion or a preference for other topics. It's not just that those other areas are more interesting or more important. It's that religion is bad—stigmatizing, in fact. When it comes to academic records, "religion is sticky" as sociologist of religion Rick Moore says. I may go even further and say "radioactive." Consequently, we're preparing students for anti-religion bias.

Scientists are not free from bias. In fact, "science" is best thought of as a disciplined way of thinking and set of practices emerging from our recognition that all human beings—scientists very much included—suffer from various forms of bias. Science has to be learned because it requires an unnatural and counterintuitive way of thinking. Our *natural* bent is toward confirmation bias, group-think, gambler's fallacies, availability heuristics, and dozens of other mental shortcuts that Homo sapiens developed to survive. And the commitment to real science isn't just about learning techniques; it's an allegiance to a way of building knowledge. That allegiance demands nothing less than the honesty to recognize our own biases, the diligence to account for those biases with systematic and transparent methods, the humility to have our biases pointed out when necessary, and the courage to change.[2]

In his 2021 book *How Social Science Got Better*, political scientist Matt Grossmann boils down most of our improvement in the social sciences to improvements in diagnosing and accounting for our own biases, individually and institutionally. Confronting and addressing our biases, in other words, is *collectively* redemptive. Not only do our particular research projects benefit when observers point out some flaws in our thinking and systems, we also learn something about ourselves. We learn ways we didn't know we were being influenced. And that opens up the possibility of improvement. In perhaps the most beautiful description of social science's promise, the late sociologist Peter Berger compared us all (yes, including academics) to puppets being moved by society's strings. "Unlike the puppets," he explained, "we have the possibility of stopping in our movements, looking up and perceiving the machinery by which we have been moved." Berger urges us to welcome these realizations, for "In this act lies the first step toward freedom."[3]

Social science departments and the institutions that fund them must recognize some not-so-hidden biases when it comes to the study of religion. And they must have the courage to change. These prejudices may be conscious or unconscious, but mounds of research show they are nonetheless real and pernicious. They should be worrisome. Not only because they violate the spirit of intellectual integrity in recognizing and dispatching unfair bias whenever possible (our very creed). And not only because they cause us to ignore or profoundly misunderstand important social and political dynamics (our job). Both those reasons should be plenty to cause us to rethink our hiring and funding practices and the kinds of research we consider important. But our prejudices when it comes to the scientific study of religion, and religion scholars in general, also causes us to systematically ignore historically marginalized groups. This structurally perpetuates privilege.

Our unwillingness to recognize our own biases here, in other words, is about more than a benign disinterest in religion. It reveals a corruption of sorts. The purity of academic social science itself is at stake. In recognizing and correcting our anti-religion bias, and making room for the scientific study of religion, we help redeem the promise of science itself.

The "Bad Kind" of Me-Search

Scholars know full well that our intellectual interests, like our hobbies and lovers, don't just materialize from nowhere. On the contrary, the activities, relationships, and topics that consume us are often the ones that are most readily available in our social context. If we've got the fever for fantasy football or board games or scrapbooking, we likely caught the infection from family or close friends. Contrary to the Hollywood storylines filled with unlikely couples, our "soul mates" usually turn out to be those with whom we already share almost everything in common. And when we give ourselves to a life of research, like Emily, my prospective graduate student, we tend to study things that are relevant to us personally.[4]

My story is no different. As I shared in Chapter 1, my dissertation focused on a movement among evangelical Christians to promote child adoption and foster care. I found this topic interesting because I also had a personal connection to adoption and evangelicalism: both my sisters were adopted by my evangelical parents back in the 1980s. But as I read dozens of academic books and research articles on adoption, I discovered that in almost every case, the authors of these studies had adoption somewhere in their personal experience. Most often they themselves were adoptive parents. In other cases, they were adoptees. The tendency for adoption scholars to have some personal connection to adoption is so common that I find, unless I'm told otherwise, I now assume it. Even if the research is rigorous. No matter what the findings show. I assume professional academics writing about child adoption have adoption somewhere in their own personal story, and they likely have strong personal opinions that may be shaped by a combination of those experiences and their research.

It's only natural for us to assume the same about other academic topics of interest. If someone does extensive research on Muslim teenagers navigating the challenges of being regular American kids and good Muslims, I wonder where the interest comes from. In the case of professor John O'Brien's award-winning book on that topic, *Keeping It Halal*, he actually is a Muslim convert. If someone writes a book about the experiences of gay student activism at Christian colleges, I wonder what made that topic relevant for them personally. In the case of Jonathan Coley, who wrote the book *Gay on God's Campus*, he is a gay man who attended an evangelical Baptist college in the Deep South.[5]

There's a paradox here, however. On the one hand, academics are well aware most of us are doing what's often pejoratively called "me-search." We're often interested in issues that intersect with our own life experiences. Even as the German sociologist Max Weber argued for "value free" social science, he conceded that each scientist is compelled by "the demon who holds the fibers of his very life." By that he meant some deeper, a priori set of values that drive their passionate inquiry.[6] And yet, we sincerely want to conduct research that is persuasive and grounded in empirical facts. No social scientist worth a damn wants to fabricate pseudoscientific opinion pieces that are riddled with unconscious biases. Nor do we want our research perceived that way. So the fact is: most of us are doing some sort of "me-search," but we're sometimes reluctant to be open about it—and with good reason.

In 2021, clinical psychologist Andrew Devendorf and his colleagues surveyed a representative sample of faculty, graduate students, and postdoctoral fellows associated with North American psychology departments. They found roughly 55% of their sample conducted what they called "self-relevant research," which was basically research conducted by anyone who has some personal connection to that topic. "Me-search," in other words. Of this group, over 4 out of 5 had a personal connection to their research before starting it. They also found psychology faculty and trainees who were sexual or racial minorities or who had suffered mental health problems themselves were more likely to conduct "self-relevant research." Did this influence how others evaluated their work? Absolutely. Respondents were more likely to rate those who conducted self-relevant research as more biased, selfish, and having bad judgment compared to those who had no personal connection to their research topics.[7] These findings affirm both our expectations and fears: social scientists tend to study personally relevant topics and, for most, the topic was personally relevant before they started the research. But despite that fact, me-search gets dismissed as shoddy scholarship.

But there's a catch. We don't distrust *all* me-search. Whether we view a scholar's self-relevant research as biased and untrustworthy hinges on what we think about the research topic itself. Social psychologist Marlene Sophie Altenmuller and her colleagues conducted several experiments in which they tested how adults feel about research when the scholar had some sort of personal connection to the topic. In one example, they showed participants a scholar who self-identified as homosexual and was studying LGBTQ+ topics. And for a less socially controversial example (at least outside of the BBQ loving American South), they asked about a vegan studying vegan lifestyles. For both examples, they found whether participants viewed the me-search positively or negatively depended largely on their attitudes toward the topic. When participants held negative views toward LGBTQ issues or veganism, they viewed the research of scholars personally affected by those topics more negatively. But if they had positive views toward those topics, they viewed the self-relevant research as more trustworthy. In fact, when participants already held positive views of the research topic, learning the scholar was personally affected by their research made the participants less critical of the entire field of research on that topic.[8]

So we're distrustful of "me-search," but specifically the me-search about topics we already feel negatively toward. That matters for the secular academy and scientific research on religion. As numerous studies show, and I'll demonstrate later in the chapter, academics tend to be a relatively secular bunch. And many (though certainly not all) academics are dismissive if not downright contemptuous of religion itself.[9] If many academics already tend to hold mostly negative attitudes toward religion as a phenomenon, what do they think about those who study it? Specifically, what might they think about those who study religion if they assume such scholars have some personal connection to it? Drawing these connections may help us understand why religion research is not only valued less but also can be actively stigmatized.

Psychologist Kimberly Rios has been studying religious identity within the context of academic science for years. Recounting her experiences, she explained, "Perhaps the number-one question I encounter from people who learn I study psychology of religion is 'Are you religious?' In other words, they assume my research is 'me-search.'" Other interactions, she recalled, were downright negative. Years back she tried to publish an article on stereotype threat among Christians in science, which ultimately landed in a top-ranked social psychology journal. However, an earlier reviewer questioned whether the article contributed anything to the psychology of Christians "except to provide solid evidence to support the well-discussed stereotype that Christianity and science don't mix." This was a puzzling statement considering her study *actually* showed that differences in scientific performance between Christians and non-Christians disappears when the negative stereotype is directly debunked. (The reviewer seemed to be displaying their own blind prejudice, in other words.) Other colleagues recounted the psychology of religion being dismissed as "dumb." And still others relayed stories similar to mine and Emily's at the beginning of this chapter. Their advisors were directing their students toward research areas like gender and race and away from religion.

Curious about these experiences, Rios and her graduate student Zachary Roth conducted an experiment in which they randomly assigned hundreds of psychology researchers to answer questions about five areas of social and personality psychology: religion/spirituality, political psychology, gender, attitudes and persuasion, or judgment and decision-making. The researchers first asked psychology faculty and trainees to associate a long list of characteristics with scholars working in the assigned subfield. The characteristics included those related to social identities (e.g., "liberal," "conservative," "religious," "racial minority") and intellectual rigor (e.g., "intelligent," "subjective"). Rios and Roth also had participants answer questions about whether research in given areas of psychology were mainstream, rigorous, and should be published in the top journals in social and personality psychology.

Just as Rios's anecdotes would lead us to expect, psychology researchers scored research on religion or spirituality as less mainstream, less rigorous, and less deserving of space in top psychology journals compared to all the other areas of psychology. Moreover, participants were more likely to associate religion specialists with characteristics like "religious" and "subjective." Psychology faculty and trainees were also less likely to associate religion researchers with words like "intelligent" compared to researchers in other areas of psychology. And religion research didn't seem to be a proxy for conservatism, because participants weren't more likely to associate religion specialists with being "conservative" compared to psychologists in other areas. Instead, the negative perception was truly about those who study religion.[10]

I decided to replicate and extend this study with my own survey experiment focusing on sociologists. In September 2022, I recruited 536 sociology faculty, postdocs, and graduate students to take a survey that was very similar to the one created by Rios and Roth. For my survey, I randomly assigned participants to one of six different subfields within sociology: religion, economic sociology, sociology of education, race and ethnicity, gender and sexuality, and the sociology of population or demography. I chose these other subfields because they are often well represented either in the discipline as a whole (race and ethnicity, gender and sexuality) and/or at elite departments (economic sociology, sociology of education, demography). I also added several questions about whether high-ranking sociology departments should have scholars who study a particular subfield, whether *all* sociology departments should have sociologists who specialize in that subfield, and whether undergraduates would be interested in taking courses in that subfield.

What did I find? Unlike Rios and Roth, I didn't find meaningful differences between subfields in terms of how sociologists rated them according to rigor or worthiness to be in the top journals or departments, or in how interested undergraduates would be in such courses. It was abundantly clear, however, that religion is marginal within the discipline compared to the other subfields and optional as an area of expertise for faculty. Figure 5.1 shows that nearly 30% fewer sociologists agree that religion is a mainstream part of sociology compared to every other subfield. Further, like economic sociology and demography, far fewer sociologists agree that all sociology departments should have faculty with expertise in religion compared to education, race and ethnicity, or gender and sexuality. Thus, even if religious research isn't openly regarded as less rigorous or worthy of prestige, sociologists still view religion as outside of mainstream sociology. At best, sociologists may

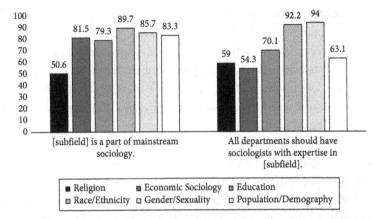

Figure 5.1. Percentage of sociologists who said a particular subfield was mainstream or all departments should have sociologists with expertise in that area.

Source: 2022 Sociologists across Subfields Survey.

view religion as a "boutique" subfield that sociology departments only have when they're already loaded with other more "bread and butter" subfields.

And I should also explain that these numbers aren't skewed by sociologists of religion in the sample who are overly sensitive about being marginalized within the discipline. Of the sociologists who were randomly assigned religion as a subfield, only 8% were sociologists who specialize in religion, and they scored similarly to everyone else.

But what about the characteristics sociologists associate with religion specialists? Just like Rios and Roth, I found the most common characteristic that sociology faculty and trainees associate with sociologists of religion is being themselves "religious." In fact, a whopping 64% of those who were randomly assigned to evaluate religion as a subfield characterized sociologists who study religion as "religious." Interestingly, a nontrivial number of sociology faculty and trainees (19.3%) also associated sociologists

who study religion with being "nonreligious." And 10% of sociology researchers indicated both "religious" and "nonreligious"
as characteristics. What this means is that nearly three-quarters of
sociologists who evaluated religion as a subfield associated religion
specialists with some sort of "me-search"—that they're studying religion because their lives are somehow oriented around embracing
or rejecting religion.

But unlike Rios and Roth, I also found that a higher percentage
of sociologists characterized sociologists of religion as "conservative" (35%) compared to any other subfield. (Economic sociology
was slightly less likely to be associated with conservatism, but not
to a statistically significant degree.) Moreover, 33% of sociologists
who evaluated religion characterized sociologists in this subfield as
both "conservative" and "religious."

Is there any truth to either of these assumptions? Before I answer, we should keep in mind that whether someone is personally
religious or not gives us no ethically justifiable reason to assume
they are more or less qualified as social scientists. To assume that
characteristic somehow marks them as suspect reflects the very
anti-religion bias social scientists of religion fear. But the fact is,
sociologists who study religion (my sample included) are indeed
more likely to be religiously affiliated than their counterparts.[11]
And this shouldn't surprise us. Self-relevant research is common
and expected. Such sociologists in my sample are not conservatives,
however. Of those who indicated they specialize in religion,
85% identified as liberal or very liberal, 9% were moderate, less
than 6% were conservative, and none were very conservative. In
terms of party identification, 78% of those specializing in religion
identified with the Democratic Party, 19% were independent, less
than 4% identified as leaning Republican, and none were strong
Republicans. Thus while it is true that a disproportionate percentage of sociologists in my survey who study religion are themselves religious, they embrace neither the Republican Party nor a
conservative ideological identity.

But regardless of the actual characteristics of sociologists of religion, peer assumptions are what matter. Because it turns out those assumptions are quite relevant for how sociologists evaluated the centrality and rigor of religious research within the discipline.

Figure 5.2 shows the difference in scores for sociologists of religion on measures of centrality to the discipline and scientific rigor by whether or not their peers characterized them as "religious" or "conservative." In Panel A, we see sociologists who thought of colleagues who study religion as "religious" were clearly less likely to view them as doing sociology that is rigorous, deserving of space in the top journals or departments, or to even think undergraduates would be interested in taking their courses. Panel B shows nearly identical patterns by whether sociologists considered those who study religion as "conservative."

And it's important to note that it's not the idea of bias or "me-search" that leads sociologists to downgrade religion specialists. The problem is that it's the wrong kind of bias. For example, when I look at scores by whether sociologists characterize religion specialists as "liberal" (17%) or "nonreligious" (19%), there was no significant difference in whether they considered such research rigorous, deserving of placement in top journals or departments, or interesting to undergrads. Moreover, participants quite often characterized specialists in other subfields like gender/sexuality or race/ethnicity as "activist" or as having some identity that made the research personally relevant for them, like being female or a racial minority. Yet they didn't downgrade those subfields as a result. Rather it is when sociologists view religion specialists as "religious" and/or "conservative" that their research is discounted.[12]

These are findings that systematically verify anecdotes that could be recounted by any number of sociologists, political scientists, and psychologists who study religion. Religion scholars are assumed to be doing "me-search," which happens to be viewed negatively, particularly when people feel negatively toward the topic being studied. And not only are those who study religion suspected of

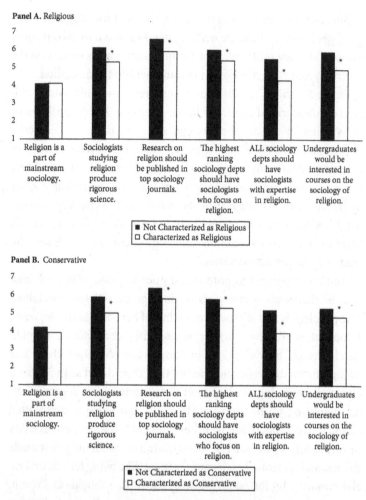

Figure 5.2. Scores on measures of centrality and scientific rigor for the sociology of religion by whether sociologists of religion are characterized as "religious" or "conservative."

* Indicates a statistically significant difference between comparison groups at the .05 level.

Source: 2022 Sociologists across Subfields Survey.

being religious and conservative, among those who assume this to be the case, they presume religion specialists are lower-class social scientists. This isn't benign disinterest. This is professional stigma directed toward those who even approach religion as a topic.

Is There Open Discrimination?

If social scientists openly devalue religion research and stereotype religion specialists as less intelligent, more religious, more conservative, and more biased, we shouldn't be surprised that job boards for academic psychologists, sociologists, and political scientists only rarely search for religion scholars. In my academic field of sociology, for example, there are almost never any job searches for sociologists of religion explicitly. Religion may be mentioned in the advertisement as one possible area of interest among others, but even that is fleetingly rare.

Figure 5.3 shows the total number of listings for the top-10 area specializations most often listed in job advertisements on the American Sociological Association jobs board from 2016 to 2022. I've listed those top-10 areas alongside religion, which is never anywhere near the top specializations listed. And I would reiterate, though religion was apparently listed among areas of interest 39 times since 2016 (and I was shocked to read it was that frequent), the number of times searches were actually conducted for that specialization in particular could be counted on one hand. And I would also point out during the 2020 job cycle, when searches were more scarce because of the COVID-19 pandemic, religion was listed zero times.

My point in illustrating the disparity isn't to imply that religion is more important than, say, "Racial and Ethnic Relations." But religion being listed 39 times to the latter's 401 times (over a 10-fold difference) is a remarkable disparity considering that the vast majority of Americans still identify with a religious tradition and

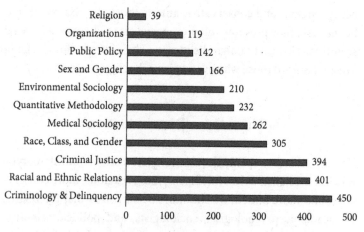

Figure 5.3. Total number of listings for each specialization on the American Sociological Association Jobs Board, 2016–2022.
Source: American Sociological Association Published Reports, 2016–2023.

say they pray weekly, believe the Bible is true, and that religion is at least fairly important to them. It's also difficult to conceive that student interest in taking classes on formal organizations or environmental sociology would be over three times greater than their interest in courses on religion. These differences instead seem to reflect the preferences of sociologists themselves.

But is there open discrimination against religion scholars? Here's where the tendency to assume research interests are "me-search" and specifically to stereotype religion scholars as themselves religious or conservative should give us greater cause for worry. There is a growing body of research that religious persons in science fields feel targeted as well as some research showing social scientists really would discriminate against such job applicants if they had the chance. And whether scholars of religion are in fact religious is irrelevant if their research interests stereotype them as such.

Studies show religious graduate students and professors in fields like biology or physics are more likely to feel discriminated against because of their faith compared to those who are unaffiliated.[13] Regardless of whether they are in fact being discriminated against, perceptions of discrimination are themselves a problem because they may lead to talented persons selecting themselves out of science majors and careers. And because stereotypes are lousy indicators of applicants' potential contributions, the possibility of religious persons selecting themselves out of scientific fields is just as ethically problematic as women, people of color, or queer persons self-selecting out of STEM fields for fear of discrimination. Moreover, there's also some evidence that negative stereotypes against religious persons may influence scientific performance. Psychologist Kimberly Rios and her colleagues found in a series of experiments that when Christians were exposed to stereotypes about their incompetence in science, they not only became less interested in science but also underperformed in science-related tasks.[14] (Similar studies have shown that racial minorities underperform in academic tasks when they are made cognizant of racist stereotypes about intelligence.[15])

But there's evidence to suggest the problem goes beyond perceptions. Rios and her colleagues, for example, found that non-Christians in their study openly endorsed stereotypes about Christians being less competent in science. Could such stereotypes lead to fewer opportunities in scientific fields for those perceived to be religious, or Christians specifically? Biologist Elizabeth Barnes and her colleagues conducted a survey experiment in which they presented biology professors with various resumes and applications for work in their lab. They found professors rated a student who went on a mission trip with Campus Crusade for Christ as less hirable, less competent, and less likable than a student who did not reveal a Christian identity.[16]

But are they less likely to get the job? To test whether businesses are actually discriminating against religious applicants, researchers have conducted field experiments called "audit studies" in which they change details on applications to see whether applicants who include indicators of a religious background are less likely to get the call-back or interview.[17] Unfortunately, such experiments are nearly impossible to do in academia. Academic departments require far too much information about candidates to simply change a few details on resumes. Moreover, academic disciplines are a small world. And hiring committees would likely be outraged to discover their colleagues at another university wasted their time by sending out fake resumes.[18] So in 2008 sociologist George Yancey did the next best thing—he tested whether his fellow academics said they *would* discriminate against certain candidates if they had opportunity.

Like many survey experiments, Yancey wanted to avoid social desirability bias that might creep in if participants knew they were being evaluated on their prejudices. So he distributed a survey to academic departments under the guise of assessing "collegiality." He asked professional academics who completed the survey whether they would be more or less likely to support hiring a person if they learned the candidate was a _____. Yancey then listed a number of identities and group memberships. This is an enlightening question, because there are numerous things we are forbidden to ask about in professional interviews. This is to keep us from discriminating against candidates who hold characteristics that should not affect a candidate's ability to teach courses, conduct research, and contribute to department life (family status, religious identity, sexual orientation, etc.). Nonetheless, these characteristics matter to us socially. As sociologist Lauren Rivera shows, hiring often works out like a collective exercise in "cultural matching" in which our desire to hire people who are like us culturally often outweighs our evaluations of their objective skills and qualifications.[19]

What did Yancey learn about who academics were inclined to discriminate against? Among the social scientists, being a fundamentalist or evangelical were the most damning identities. Over 67% of anthropologists said learning a job applicant was a fundamentalist would hurt their candidacy. Majorities of history, physics, English, and philosophy faculty also said being a fundamentalist would hurt their chances. Roughly half of sociologists said the same. Evangelical candidates only fared slightly better. About 59% of anthropologists said being an evangelical would hurt someone's job chances, as did 53% of English faculty, and nearly 40% of political scientists, physicists, and sociologists. But lest you think these faculty were just using religion as some sort of proxy for Republicans, Yancey asked about Republicans too. And they weren't rated nearly as low as fundamentalists or evangelicals. That means those conservative Christian identities represent something scarier than simply being a Republican (at least in 2008, when Yancey did the survey). They represent a perceived cultural backwardness that a large percentage of professional academics (and even majorities in some departments) would weed out if they got the chance.

This is bias. And to the extent that admissions and hiring committees catch signals of religious conservatism, and that discovery disadvantages the applicant, that is the definition of discrimination. This one hits close to home for me. The education portion of my CV shows a seminary degree, already outing myself as having some sort of Christian background. But even worse, that degree is from a flagship evangelical school where I graduated top of my class. At no time during my academic career have I considered myself conservative or Republican. Nor would my research suggest some sort of pro-conservative or evangelical bias if hiring committees bothered to read it. But my background and frankly many of my most cherished relationships scream "devout evangelical." I've often wondered: have hiring committees looked at my CV, seen my evangelical seminary degree, and decided to look elsewhere, just in case?

It should be no surprise that studies find graduate students with religious beliefs and backgrounds intentionally conceal their identities to avoid the discrimination they realistically could face.[20] I've seen this firsthand. Though a certain "screw them" attitude led me to keep my seminary degree on my CV when I was applying for academic jobs, I had friends who chose otherwise. Several of them even removed their seminary degrees from their vitae. They weren't trying to deceive. But they reasoned that it didn't contribute any relevant information to their educational history hiring departments would be justified in considering. In other words, these candidates knew religious signals would be a strike against them, so they removed them. They also happened to get great jobs.

Potential anti-religion bias and discrimination is bad enough. But it's also a bias that almost certainly extends beyond the target. It's already been shown that both psychologists and sociologists of religion are more likely to be characterized as religious, whether they are in fact religious or not. To the extent that admissions and hiring committees draw negative conclusions about applicants from their very research interests, even the fact that scholars focus on religion in their research could mark them.

Sociologist Rick Moore (who happens to be an atheist) shared with me that "I don't know if others had this experience, but I often felt that studying religion was like a scarlet letter. I could talk *forever* about my work on culture and cognition but still feel I was reduced to simply being a 'religion guy' because that's where my empirical work was. To be clear this didn't happen all the time, but I can think of specific examples where my studying religion seemed to override other aspects of my research for some people." From what Rick describes, religion research becomes what the late sociologist Howard Becker called a stigmatizing "master status trait." It overrides other attributes such that individuals only view persons in terms of that stigmatized label.[21] To the extent this happens because someone's research interests trigger contempt or the fear of hiring the "wrong kind" of social scientist, that is an outrage.

And there's another way such bias extends beyond the target. Religious identities and interests in religion aren't limited to white, formerly evangelical men. In fact, it's likely that anti-religion bias disproportionately affects scholars of color and women just as it causes us to ignore core features of their social worlds.

The Flipside of Me-Search

There is a more subtle form of anti-religion bias in academia that on the surface feels more benign than stereotypes about religion scholarship being shoddy or religion scholars being more religious—and shoddy. It is the flipside of me-search. Scholars tend to be more fascinated by issues that are relevant to them personally. And they also seem to disregard topics they find personally irrelevant.[22] But just as me-search reflects a clear example of one sort of bias ("This happened to me and therefore it is important."), we fail to recognize how equally biased it is to conclude that whole areas of interest are better left ignored because we personally don't find them relevant. But this is the way we perpetuate privilege.

The National Center for Educational Statistics reports that about 4 in 10 college professors are white, non-Hispanic men. This is already disproportionate to their share of the US population (3 in 10). But white, non-Hispanic men also currently make up over half (51%) of academics at the rank of full professor. At the level of college administration, the disparity is even worse. The vast majority of college presidents and provosts (those who distribute the money) have historically been and still remain disproportionately white and male.[23] What this means is that those who hold the most authority on university campuses, and whose opinions carry the most weight when it comes to the direction of the university or their particular department, are white men. This may be changing gradually as college faculty and administration are diversifying, but it remains the case today.[24]

This matters for more reasons than race and gender disparities, because this particular population (highly educated white men) is also among the most secular populations in the country. This has been the case for some time. According to data from the 2005 Religion Among Academic Scientists survey, over half of sociologists, political scientists, psychologists, and economists were either atheists or agnostics. And these numbers grow to over 60% when looking at white men. We see similar secularity in other studies of scientists even without taking into account race and gender. Pew Research Center conducted a 2014 survey of over 3,700 members of the American Academy of Arts and Sciences and found that over half were religiously unaffiliated and less than one-third identified as any kind of Christian. In 2015, sociologist Elaine Howard Ecklund conducted a survey of biologists and physicists in the United States. She found only 30% identified as religious at all compared to well over twice that percentage (67%) of the American population as a whole.

Let's focus on sociologists as they compare to the rest of the country. The first two columns in Table 5.1 show the religious self-identification of the sociologists in Elaine Ecklund's 2005 Religion Among Academic Scientists (RAAS) survey and those sociology faculty and trainees in my 2022 survey. Though my survey isn't a random sample, the religion numbers are quite similar to those in Ecklund's earlier random sample of sociologists in university positions. The only major difference is Ecklund's sample has a substantially higher percentage of Jewish sociologists. And my sample has a somewhat higher percentage of those who are unaffiliated, though this is pulled upward by the greater irreligiosity of graduate students in the sample. Faculty are actually slightly more likely to be affiliated, likely reflecting their membership in a comparatively more religious cohort of Americans. Table 5.1 also compares these numbers to those in the general population. There are numerous data sets that could be used for that purpose, but Pew Research Center's 2021 American Trends Panel Survey (wave 84) provides an enormous sample (roughly 12,000 adults) that I've used more than once in this book already. Thus for consistency's sake, I'll use this survey.

Table 5.1. Religious Identification of Sociologists and American Adults

| | Sociologists | | | All Americans | | | |
	RAAS (2005)	SAS (2022)	Total	White	Black	Hispanic	Asian
Conservative Protestant	1.6	2.8	25.7	26	45	16.3	7.2
Liberal Protestant	11.7	15.3	15.6	17.5	23.5	6.4	4.5
Catholic	8.6	5.1	21	19	4	45.4	18.1
Jewish	18.8	6	1.6	2.4	.1	.8	0
Muslim	.8	1.3	.7	.3	.9	0	6.6
Other Religious Group	6.2	4.9	7.5	6.3	4.8	5.6	22.9
Unaffiliated	52.3	64.4	27.8	28.5	21.7	25.5	40.7
Atheist	31.3	27	4.5	5.9	.4	2.2	5.4
Agnostic	25.8	19.3	5.6	6.3	1.7	4.1	10.1
Nothing in Particular		18.1	17.7	16.3	19.6	19.2	25.2

Source: Religion Among Academic Scientists Survey (2005); Sociology Across Subfields Survey (September 2022); 2021 American Trends Panel Survey, Wave 84 (March 2021).

Comparing sociologists and average Americans, sociologists are considerably less Christian, primarily because there are significantly fewer sociology faculty or trainees who are conservative Protestants or Catholics. The percentage of liberal Protestants among sociologists in my sample is nearly identical with that of the general population, and most particularly, white and Black Americans. Minority religious groups like Jews and Muslims were also more prominently represented among sociologists. But where the sociologists in my sample clearly stand out from the general population is the percentage of seculars. Approaching one-half (46.3%) of my survey identified as atheist (27%) or agnostic (19.3%). In addition to those who identified as "nothing in particular" (18.1%), that means nearly two-thirds of these sociologists (64.4%) are religiously unaffiliated. Though the percentage of Americans who are "nothing in particular" are quite similar, the numbers for atheists and agnostics aren't anywhere in the ballpark. The highest group is Asians at 15.5% atheist or agnostic, followed by whites at 12%.

If my sample of sociologists is anywhere in the neighborhood of representing the discipline as a whole (and quite frankly these numbers certainly pass the smell test as someone in the discipline), the vast majority of sociology faculty, grad students, and postdocs are secular persons, with well under 10% identifying with anything close to conservative Christianity. In fact, there is some evidence in the data that the discipline itself is becoming even more secular. In Figure 5.4, I look at the percentage of sociologists in the sample who identify with a Christian tradition or with a more secular identity (atheist, agnostic, nothing in particular). The tenured senior

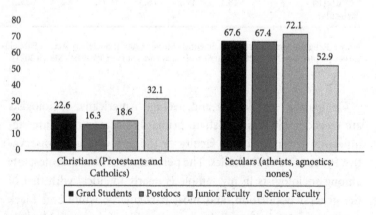

Figure 5.4. Percentage of Christian and secular sociologists by academic position.
Source: 2022 Sociology across Subfields Survey (September 2022).

faculty in the sample are still relatively secular by the standards of the general population, but there tend to be more Christians (almost all liberal Protestants) among them compared to early-career sociologists. Meanwhile, those sociologists either in training or moving through the pipeline are considerably more secular, with about a 15%–20% difference. Indeed, a full 50% of grad students and postdocs in the sample are atheists or agnostics.

Flipping around our assumptions about me-search, it should be unsurprising that departments run by an increasingly secular demographic would be skeptical about religion's relevance.[25] And as we observed earlier, there is evidence that this particularly secular crowd may view religion not merely with disinterest but outright contempt. Not only is this problematic in the way that all negative stereotypes are problematic, but it potentially reflects an "our kind of people" bias. That sort of bias almost certainly extends beyond religion itself (as if religion could be divorced from the people who identify with it and practice it) to those who also tend to be more religious on average—racial minorities and women.

In a recent survey of graduate students across multiple disciplines, sociologist Christopher Scheitle and his colleagues found that religious graduate students perceived greater discrimination against them because of their religion compared to irreligious students. But this wasn't just a situation in which white evangelical conservatives were particularly sensitive and consumed with persecution complexes. On the contrary, it was graduate students *of color* who felt discriminated against due to their religion. In fact, Scheitle and his colleagues found that perceptions of religious discrimination powerfully overlapped with perceptions of racial and gender discrimination. This means that people who are made to feel like outsiders because of their religious identity also tend to feel like outsiders because of their racial and gender identity.[26] We don't just have an anti-religion bias problem. We have what social psychologists call a "prototypicality" problem in which those who "belong" are those most representative of the dominant group—secular, white, men. This sort of bias also leads us to continue overlooking populations all too often ignored in our own research.

In one of the most famous studies of the past 15 years (cited over 15,000 times as I write this), psychologist Joseph Henrich and his colleagues argue that behavioral scientists have based almost all of their research on samples drawn from Western, Educated, Industrialized, Rich, and Democratic (WEIRD) societies. And most of those samples are undergraduates in such societies who make the most readily available participants for our experiments. Henrich and his team show that not only do these populations differ from others around the world, *the WEIRD populations are the outliers*. In other words, not only do behavioral scientists incorrectly generalize from one unique population, they often choose the worst population from which to generalize![27]

In an even more famous work published just after Henrich's study, moral psychologist Jonathan Haidt argued in his bestseller *The Righteous Mind* that white secular academics (those who most represent these WEIRD societies) often ignore the fact that those who grew up in more traditional, non-WEIRD societies outnumber them considerably. But such academics also have a difficult time understanding that it is *they* who are the global outliers on issues like religion, tradition, authority, and social purity.[28] The result is that secular behavioral scientists end up doing bad science at best (ignoring a tremendous percentage of the human population) and at worst end up surrounding themselves with like-minded community members who reproduce the same biases and blindspots.

Conclusion

None of this is to argue that political science, psychology, and sociology departments need to hire more religious fundamentalists, traditional Christians, or members of any particular religious group. This isn't one more argument for "ideological diversity" on college campuses. To be clear, I would *not* encourage hiring social scientists who subscribe to theories of racial eugenics or that certain segments of the population should be denied rights to marriage, child adoption, healthcare, or any other civil rights on the basis of some presumed harm to civilization. But my opposition to hiring such academics wouldn't be because they are religious per se. Rather, their views represent junk science and have no place in a secular academy, whether the one who holds them is religious or not. Similarly, I'm also not suggesting all social scientists of religion even deserve jobs. Some may be insufferable jerks. Others haven't published that combination of quality and quantity of research that would merit a tenure-track job. But neither of these issues would stem from the fact that they study religion.

I'm also not arguing that social science departments should hire for religion so often that "religion" becomes listed on the ASA jobs board over 50 times per year the way specialties like "criminology," "criminal justice," and "racial and ethnic relations" are. Certainly, I believe social science departments, for their own sakes, should be more interested in hiring religion specialists. And I think I've shown this matters now more than ever, given the religious realities I've described in the previous chapters. Yet I acknowledge there are a variety of factors that go into why certain areas of specialization need more professors than others. Criminology and criminal justice majors, for example, make up an enormous portion of majors in my own department. These are also directly applicable majors for law enforcement and legal practice. Consequently, more scholars in this area are needed. So too racial inequality is not only a fundamental aspect of American life that social scientists are obligated to understand, but the topic intersects with a variety of subfields within our discipline, making scholars in this area particularly useful.

My foundational premise for this chapter is simply the fact that science is improved by recognizing and addressing our biases. As political scientist Matt Grossmann explains, "Researching and managing bias within the scientific community is the unheralded engine of progress."[29] And the social sciences in particular should recognize what social scientists of religion have known for decades. Academics are a relatively secular population and there's evidence that not only do they fail to recognize religion's importance to most of the country and the world, they also tend to unfairly view religion specialists as subpar academics and suspect they're engaged in the "bad kind" of me-search.

Helping graduate students think strategically about their research trajectory is good and necessary. But I shouldn't have to coach my graduate students through hiding their research interests. I shouldn't have to help them think through scrubbing their CV of any indication they could still have religious leanings themselves. Scholars who are racial minorities and/or women already face enough systemic disadvantages when it comes to surviving and thriving in academia. They shouldn't also have to worry that their religious identities (or even signals of religious identities) could be an additional strike against them.

Much of the anti-religion bias we see in the social sciences likely stems from unconscious ethnocentrism. But some of it, I fear, stems from conscious antipathy toward religion and religious people. Each of these tendencies needs to be checked because it corrupts science itself in the name of defending it. Leaning into the scientific study of religion, in other words, not only immediately increases our relevance but also corrects our blindspots and helps fulfill the promise of the social sciences.

6

Fulfilling the Promise

What Religion Scholars Owe the Public

When I first pitched the idea for this book to my longtime editor, I apparently hadn't done an effective job of helping him catch the vision. In fact, his initial response was something like, "I don't think the solution to our national problems will be to get the Christian right to start reading the *Journal for the Scientific Study of Religion*." That wasn't exactly my goal, but his point stuck with me. The Christian right, along with the majority of American adults, would never read our academic journals. Most journals are paywalled with exorbitant subscription fees that only university libraries will pay. Much of their content is irrelevant to issues average people care about. And our studies are written to other scholars in jargony language that assumes common methodological knowledge. As a result, the people who know anything about our work will tend to be those most like us in terms of education and culture.

Let me give you an example that is both sobering and humbling for a scholar who's worked hard to successfully reach broader audiences with my research, or so I thought. Think about a concept that surely everyone's heard about these days: "Christian nationalism." It seems I can't go anywhere without seeing the phrase thrown around on social media or the latest book or article. On our own, my coauthors and I have literally published dozens of peer-reviewed studies on the topic, and there seems to be a whole subfield of Christian nationalism scholarship emerging across sociology, political science, and psychology. But who *really* knows about that term? In the latter half of 2022, Pew Research Center

Religion for Realists. Samuel L. Perry, Oxford University Press. © Oxford University Press 2024.
DOI: 10.1093/oso/9780197672549.003.0007

and the Public Religion Research Institute both conducted surveys in which they asked Americans whether they had heard or read anything about "Christian nationalism." When I analyzed both surveys, I found the exact same pattern. Those who'd heard or read the most (or anything at all) about "Christian nationalism" were very liberal, secular Americans with postgraduate degrees who trust news sources like MSNBC, while those who'd heard or read nothing about the concept were more likely to be less educated, politically conservative Christians who trust Fox News. And a 2024 study by Pew Research Center finds these trends remain largely unchanged. It seems that despite nearly a decade of work trying to help the world understand Christian nationalism, we have largely been "preaching to the choir." Not necessarily other academics, but certainly those who would already have the most access to our kind of work, and who would need little convincing that "Christian nationalism" is problematic for society. We face a real challenge of reach and translation.[1]

But there is also a trust issue. Religious Americans tend to be more suspicious of professional academics, scientists, and professors. And as I showed in the previous chapter, some of that suspicion is justified. If social scientists tend to hold negative prejudices toward religious or conservative Americans, and evidence suggests many do, why would the latter trust much of what the former has to say about issues that are most important to them? For one, our research on religion is less likely to represent the best science. As sociologists Rodney Stark and Roger Finke explain, "[S]ocial scientists are unlikely even to grasp the human side of phenomena for which they have no empathy."[2] But as so many studies on identity-protective cognition and confirmation bias now confirm, if we're perceived as hostile, our findings will be rejected out of hand regardless of their accuracy.[3]

The argument of this book is that we all need *religion for realists*. And we need it now more than ever. Given where religion is headed in our world and how it's being used, we need to have

our understanding shaped by reliable evidence and rigorous empirical methods. But there is a barrier even more formidable than
the obstinacy of zealous anti-intellectuals or the biases of many
secular academics. Our primary challenge is a failing system based
on an orientation to academic work that has become completely
outmoded, if it ever was appropriate at all. Within this system we
congratulate ourselves for work nobody reads (or even has access
to) and scoff at those who do public-facing work (the kind that
legitimizes everything we do to a wider audience) as "popularizers"
and "self-promoters."

Scientific research is already changing all around us. Our scholarship needs to change with it. We need to change. For those of us
who presume to study religion from a scientific perspective, our
professional survival should be motivation enough. But even more
than that, the scholarly task at hand is incomplete if our data remain hidden in our hard drives when the world deserves to be able
to test our claims. Or when the work we do stays in the pages of es-
oteric journals and erudite tomes nobody reads, like the proverbial
tree falling in the forest with nobody to hear it. And it emerges still-
born if we are unwilling to earn the trust of wider audiences, but
instead take for granted that our credibility is unquestioned.

In this final chapter, I explain the challenge we face and how
religion scholars can earn a wider audience among religious and
irreligious Americans who need our work urgently. It's not with
gimmicks, flash, or self-promotion. We need a greater commitment to the people and phenomena we write about; transparency; accountability; and a permanent reorientation of why we do
what we do.

Do They Distrust Science or Scien*tists*?

Among the most tragic casualties of American polarization in the
past few decades, and one of the barriers that stand in the way of

convincing Americans with evidence-based approaches to religion, has been Americans' trust in intellectual leadership and institutions. This includes scientists, leaders in the scientific community, college professors, universities, and higher education generally. As I demonstrated in the previous chapter, there are sadly legitimate reasons for some of this distrust. And I'll elaborate on other reasons in a moment. But we know much of this growing distrust is due to polarization because trust among political and ideological liberals has risen in the past few decades, while distrust seems almost entirely localized to religious and political conservatives.[4]

Take polling data on Americans' confidence in higher education. Among Democrats, their opinion toward higher education has stayed largely stable, and if it has declined, it seems primarily due to concerns over student loan debt. But between 2015 and 2019, Pew Research Center found the percentage of Republicans who believe universities are having a negative effect on the way things are going in our country increased 22 percentage points from 37% to 59%. Gallup showed a similar pattern in reverse: between 2015 and 2018 the percentage of Republicans saying they had confidence in higher education fell from 56% to 39%. Why has Republican confidence fallen? Among Republicans who said higher education was headed in the wrong direction, the highest percentage (nearly 4 out of 5) said "Professors are bringing their political and social views into the classroom.[5]

This tracks with broader trends in public opinion about scientists and leaders in the scientific community. Scholars have shown for over a decade now that religious and political conservatives are not necessarily hostile to science in the abstract sense. But they are noticeably more suspicious of scientists. We can see this clearly in Figure 6.1. Pew asked Americans whether they thought science had made people's lives better the past 20 years and whether they thought science would improve people's lives in the next 20 years. They also asked how much confidence they had in scientists to act in the best interests of the public. Notice there are minimal

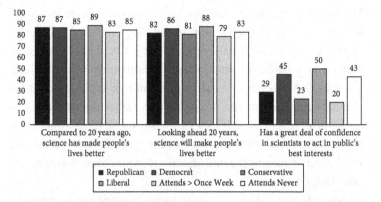

Figure 6.1. Percentage of Americans who hold certain views about science and scientists across political and religious characteristics.
Source: Pew Research Center, American Trends Panel (Wave 42, 2019).

differences across political and religious characteristics on the questions of whether science has or will make people's lives better. But there are large differences regarding trust in scientists. In the case of conservatives and the most frequent worship attendees, the percentage who say they have a great deal of confidence in scientists themselves is less than half that of liberals and those who never attend worship, respectively. Religious and political conservatives, in other words, aren't more likely to view science per se as a threat, but scientists.[6]

But a threat to what? Some sociologists argue the issue is moral authority, and more specifically, who has it. Religious and political conservatives, they argue, possibly see "science" as encroaching on religion's turf to make moral claims. And that has certainly been an argument prominent atheists like Sam Harris and Steven Pinker have made in recent years.[7]

Yet this doesn't really explain why Americans have increasingly divided over opinions toward scientists in particular, and not so much their views regarding science itself. It also doesn't explain why the distrust has been localized to certain fields of science.

Studies have shown, for instance, that conservatives are less likely to rate sociology as very scientific, but they don't make the same negative evaluations toward other social sciences like economics. Nor do they make the same negative evaluations regarding hard sciences that may directly challenge traditional biblical narratives about human origins like biology. Thus, rather than thinking in terms of coherent worldviews or theologies shaping Americans' orientations to scientific claims, the patterns make more sense if we think more in terms of basic distinctions groups draw between "us" and "them."[8]

Even deeply religious, conservative Americans understand the practical utility of science and technology in their own lives, and gladly make use of it. But the category of "scientist," along with members of other professional intellectual classes like "professor" or "academic," has become associated with religious, ideological, and partisan identities. Consequently, they are more easily categorized as friend or foe to Americans' primary sorting identities. Scientists, experts, academics, and professors are either "good guys" or they are part of the "regime" or establishment elite who want to criticize our values and indoctrinate our children. To the extent that "authority" is at stake, it isn't just authority over moral truth claims, but which group will have Authority (with a capital A). People like us? Or the shadowy leftist regime "scientists" seem to serve?

But social identities aren't the only factor at play here in figuring out how we can increase Americans' trust in the scientific study of religion. As it turns out, the relationship between group identities and Americans' trust in the work of religion scholars hinges on the reputation of professional academics more broadly. And that's good news, because it leaves open the possibility of intervention.

Let me show you what I mean. In a serendipitous event, Pew Research Center recently asked Americans how much confidence they would have in the things they heard or read from a professor of religion at a major university. Elsewhere in the same survey they also asked Americans whether they think university professors are friendly, neutral, or unfriendly toward religion. Let me stress that these questions are not measuring the same thing. The first one is asking about confidence in the work of a hypothetical religion professor, while the second is essentially trying to get a read on stereotypes involving professional academics and religion. And though the majority of Americans think that professors are neutral toward religion, strong majorities of Republicans (62%), ideological conservatives (65%), and white evangelicals (66%) say they think professors are unfriendly toward religion. How does that shape the trust these groups have in the sort of research and teaching offered by a professional religion scholar? What's clear is that social identities and stereotypes about professors in general work together.

Figure 6.2 shows the predicted percentage of Americans who say they would have at least "some" or "a lot" of confidence in the work of a hypothetical religion professor by whether they are an

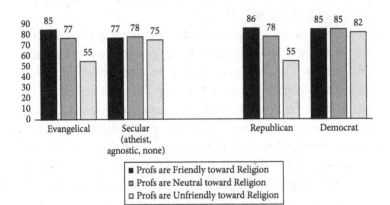

Figure 6.2. Predicted percentage of Americans who trust the work of a hypothetical religion professor.

Source: Pew Research Center, American Trends Panel (Wave 46, 2019). Results are from binary logistic regression models predicting whether someone has some/a lot of confidence in the work of a hypothetical religion professor. Controls include perceptions of professors' orientations toward religion in general, age, gender, race, education, income, region, party affiliation, ideological orientation, religious identity, and worship attendance.

evangelical Protestant or secular (atheist, agnostic, or nothing in particular) or whether they are Republicans or Democrats. Notice that for secular Americans and Democrats, their confidence in a religion scholar's work doesn't change much regardless of whether they think professors in general are friendly, neutral, or unfriendly toward religion. This is almost certainly because they don't see the work of religion professors as threatening to them personally. Whatever the religion professor says, it wouldn't be an attack on their political or religious identity.

Now look at evangelicals and Republicans. There are several important things to note. The first is that their confidence in a religion professor's work changes drastically if they perceive university professors to be more unfriendly toward religion. And this makes sense because their identities would be more sensitive to that source of threat. The more they think professors stereotypically come after "people like us" in their writing and teaching, evangelicals and Republicans will approach the work of religion scholars with greater skepticism.

But notice that if evangelicals see professors in general as neutral toward religion, their confidence in the hypothetical religion professor's research and teaching isn't substantially different from secular Americans'. In fact, among the small percentage of evangelicals who think university professors are friendly toward religion, they end up being *more* trusting of a religion professor's work on average than secular Americans. This is the same mechanism in reverse: conservative Protestants would be inclined to trust experts if they think such experts on generally on their side.

On the one hand, this reaffirms that identities matter greatly. Some Americans are more sensitive to the possibility that religion scholars could be attacking (or favoring) people like them in their teaching and research. But it also means that professional reputations matter. Even being perceived as "neutral" toward religion is enough to place evangelicals and Republicans basically on par with secular Americans and Democrats in terms of their trust in religion scholarship.[9]

Promoting Trust in Scientific Work (on Religion)

Some might object that managing our professional reputations as scholars to please religious and political conservatives is both wrong on the face of it and futile. First, readers should be aware the patterns I'm showing in Figure 6.2 go beyond Republicans and evangelicals. In the Pew data, political Independents, persons of non-Christian religious faiths, and persons who seldom attend worship services look more like the Republicans and evangelicals than the Democrats and secular Americans. What I mean is their confidence in religion scholarship also declines significantly as they perceive university professors in general to be more un-friendly toward religion. And that is the case even after I statistically hold the other key factors constant. So disregarding Americans' perceptions about our lack of scientific objectivity toward religion won't work. It's not just the opinions of white nationalists and reli-gious extremists at stake.

Readers also shouldn't misunderstand me. I'm not suggesting social scientists remain morally neutral in their orientation toward persons who oppress, abuse, or exclude others. But we do have an ethical obligation to all human beings to treat them as inher-ently worthy of information, agency, and protection. We formally agree to this, in fact, when we run our research proposals through our Institutional Review Boards. Even if we were to study Ku Klux Klan members, Neo-Nazis, religious terrorists, or murderous gang leaders, we would still be obligated to inform them of the research, gain their consent, and commit to "doing no harm" with our re-search. And these groups *should* know that such treatment is the standard among professional scholars who work with human participants.

What would we want Americans on the political and religious far-right to know about how those who conduct research will see and treat them? It is completely appropriate for them to understand that scholars operate in a separate capacity as citizens. We may hold different views from them, vote against them, and speak out when our data show why certain views or policies are problematic in light of democratic and humanistic goals. But they should not be under any impression that our research findings are the result of our deliberate efforts to gain evidence that would allow us to oppose their group. They should not think we draw our conclusions first, then find supporting data. Our goal is not to show certain groups that we are on their religious or political team. Rather we must demonstrate a commitment to principles of humanism, integrity, and scientific rigor: things we should be committed to regardless of who is watching.

Does that work? Evidence suggests it does. As I showed in Chapter 2, much evidence confirms humans tend to process social information in snap-judgments shaped by deep socialization and their identities. Yet we are obviously capable of what scholars call "bounded rationality" as individuals. And we can achieve even more concrete forms of rationality when we create environments to collectively transcend our cognitive biases. To some degree, this is the goal of all science. But the growing "open science" movement challenges us all to a higher standard. Given the virtually limitless information that can be conveyed on the Internet, we can overcome bad, biased science with better, less-biased science by increasing both transparency and accountability in our research methods. Indeed, religious and political conservatives who might otherwise be skeptical of scientists should absolutely love the norms of the open science movement, because open science is *also* inherently skeptical about scientists. It assumes all researchers are potentially ideologically motivated and self-deceived. It therefore aims to ensure better science, leaving ideologues nowhere to hide their biased work.

And implementing open science principles really does seem to increase trust, even among those most skeptical. Pew asked Americans how their confidence in scientific findings are affected when they hear the researchers' data have been made available and the study has been subject to an independent review. Figure 6.3 shows the distribution of responses across worship attendance, party affiliation, and ideological identity. Clearly there are some differences across partisan and ideological identity: Republicans and conservatives were less likely than Democrats or liberals to say these steps toward open science would increase their trust. But we shouldn't lose sight of the fact that in most cases the majority (and always at least a plurality) of any group said public access to data and independent review would increase their trust. And very few said it would decrease their trust.

The practical implications are clear here. But the inertia of institutions and late-career academics makes implementation easier said than done. Scholars who study any controversial topic that is so closely connected to Americans' cherished social identities must establish a high bar of credibility. They do this not only by expressing humanistic commitment to the safety and well-being of all people but also by following norms that are increasingly becoming established in the scientific community. These are norms like making our methods and data as transparent as possible and opening them up to scrutiny. Social science journals have already started requiring these steps in order to even publish in them. Some even require scholars to submit their data and code to editors so that independent reviewers can replicate the findings themselves.

"Preregistration" has also increasingly become the norm in experimental studies, in which scholars clearly spell out their hypotheses before they collect any data so they are actually forced to test theories rather than develop them to fit the findings post hoc.

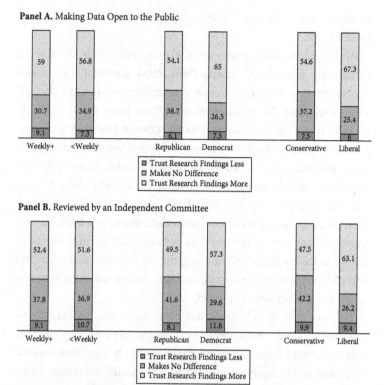

Panel A. Making Data Open to the Public

59	56.8	54.1	65	54.6	67.3
30.7	34.9	38.7	26.5	37.2	25.4
9.1	7.3	6.1	7.3	7.5	6
Weekly+	<Weekly	Republican	Democrat	Conservative	Liberal

☐ Trust Research Findings Less
☐ Makes No Difference
☐ Trust Research Findings More

Panel B. Reviewed by an Independent Committee

52.4	51.6	49.5	57.3	47.5	63.1
37.8	36.9	41.6	29.6	42.2	26.2
9.1	10.7	8.1	11.8	9.9	9.4
Weekly+	<Weekly	Republican	Democrat	Conservative	Liberal

☐ Trust Research Findings Less
☐ Makes No Difference
☐ Trust Research Findings More

Figure 6.3. Distribution of responses to changes scientists can make to increase trust in scientific studies by worship attendance, party, and ideological identity.

Source: Pew Research Center, American Trends Panel (Wave 42, 2019).

These requirements certainly create extra steps for journals and authors alike, especially if they're having to learn new software, coding skills, and data-saving techniques. But it also creates science that can transcend the crisis of legitimacy brought on by reports of fabricated data, errors in the analyses, and seminal studies that won't replicate.

Some of these steps are impossible for qualitative religious scholarship, given that we often commit to preserving confidentiality for research participants. But some aspects of open science can certainly be implemented here as well. For example, scholars often conduct in-depth interviews or participant observation with what we might call "sensitizing concepts" or theoretically informed insights about what they will expect. In fact, it's debatable whether something like "grounded theory," in which researchers develop theory completely inductively, is even possible given that we all come to the research task with some information and other biases. Thus it would make sense to preregister many qualitative studies, spelling out with some degree of specificity what the researcher expects and using findings from the data to inform those earlier expectations. This isn't the same as testing theories as in quantitative research, but it does require some forethought and transparency that would increase credibility.

And qualitative researchers can also acknowledge that some forms of data sharing are not wholly off the table. For instance, where the researcher ultimately uses quotes to illustrate a pattern in the data, they could provide the larger context for that quote in an online repository or appendix so readers could ensure it wasn't taken out of context. Related to the idea of accountability and context, qualitative research often involves researchers combing through the interview transcripts or field notes and coding them for emergent themes. An open science approach would lean toward this sort of analysis being done with multiple coders. This way, readers could have greater confidence that the conclusions were not wholly due to individual bias or idiosyncratic readings, but patterns that were apparent to all readers.

I confess that writing these past few paragraphs has been painful given that I publish with both quantitative and qualitative data, and I did not learn how to do research in an open science world. Along with most religion scholars, even most social scientists of religion, I will have to change too. But because I recognize how critical it is that average Americans understand and trust our work, I realize I must take steps toward increasing transparency and accountability in my own research, especially given the controversial nature of things I study. But there's another aspect of open science I haven't addressed yet. Before people can trust our work, they've got to know about it in the first place.

A Reorientation: Public-Facing Scholarship as the Norm

As much as I appreciate an open science approach to religion research, it doesn't go far enough. After ensuring transparency and accountability by making data available and possibly submitting work for replication, open science principles stress the need to make our research publicly available. Scholars can do this by publishing in open access journals whenever possible. And at the very least they can post free pre-prints that contain all of the content and supplemental materials even if it lacks the professional formatting of a journal. But we can do better. For any scholars who believe their work matters (and I would hope that's all of us), interested persons shouldn't just be able to stumble across our research. We should be seeking out those audiences beyond the academy.

This is potentially even more difficult for many academics than updating their technical skills and adjusting their work habits to open science standards. Academia consistently selects for smart people who know how to learn hard things. And we all acquire new skills when we have little choice, for example, if journals simply mandate certain practices. But academia doesn't always select for people who know how to translate their big ideas to broader audiences or even those who'd be inclined to do so. And this fact isn't lost on most Americans.

In a recent survey, Pew Research Center asked adults whether various characteristics described research scientists (see Figure 6.4). The good news is the vast majority of Americans associate scientists with positive characteristics. Most see them as intelligent,

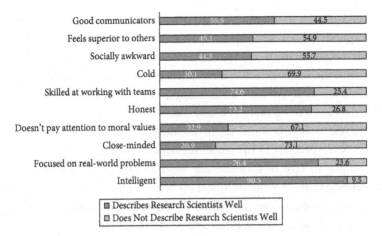

Figure 6.4. Distribution of Americans who associate various characteristics with research scientists.

Source: Pew Research Center, American Trends Panel (Wave 42, 2019).

honest, skilled at working with teams, and focused on solving real-world problems. And less than a third associated them with negative characteristics like being cold, closed-minded, or ignoring the moral values of society. But there were three characteristics about which Americans were more ambivalent. Roughly 43% of Americans (and of course even larger percentages of religious and political conservatives) felt scientists aren't good communicators, are socially awkward, and feel superior to others.

Each of these patterns suggests the potential barriers to our relaying research to the broader public are not their perceptions about our intelligence, competence, deep character problems, or even intentions. They are interpersonal barriers. And the perceptions are not off base. I can personally vouch for the social awkwardness—guilty as charged. And the perception about smugness is damning for the reason I outlined earlier. Even those adults whose identities and norms may feel threatened by our findings should see us as deeply committed to humanistic and democratic principles of equality, not as some elitist intelligentsia who feel superior to others. It's a real problem that clear majorities of Republicans, conservatives, and weekly church churchgoers say this about scientists.

But the ambivalence toward scientists as good communicators is slightly different from awkwardness or smugness, both of which reflect something more characteristic of the person. Being a good communicator is more about intentionality and skills that can be developed. Yet in the social sciences we seldom if ever receive training in how to translate our work to broader audiences. We develop skills to write technical reports for other academics. This becomes so ingrained that we have to actively resist communicating in jargon and passive voice to non-academics, to the extent we recognize we're doing it at all. And if we do gain experience in public speaking, the assumed audience is also other academics. We don't train students to speak with policymakers, business persons, clergy, or even interested soccer moms, let alone blue-collar workers. Certainly we can all improve in the techniques of communication. But scholars who study religion must first care to communicate their work to broader audiences and then learn what people want to know. And the evidence suggests people want to know how our research addresses real-world problems.

When Pew asked Americans to rank how important various kinds of scientific research was for society, nearly two-thirds (65%) indicated that "Scientific research that has immediate practical applications" is "Essential." By comparison, less than 48% classified as essential the kind of "Scientific research that advances knowledge, even if there are no immediate benefits." As a social scientist who's been described by friends as "notoriously curious," I certainly don't mean to minimize the importance of knowledge for its own sake, or knowledge that could contribute to human flourishing later. But we can't ignore the fact that the vast majority of Americans prioritize the need for immediate, practical scientific knowledge. Moreover, this is the case regardless of their religious characteristics, race, party, ideological identity, or education-level. In contrast, the only groups for which a majority extol the need for knowledge without immediate benefits are liberals, Democrats, and those with postgraduate degrees.

This doesn't mean we should change the things we study. But we should reorient our thinking toward public-facing scholarship. We should view it as the norm rather than an optional side-hustle for extroverts, popularizers, and self-promoters.

Why We All Need Religion for Realists—Now More than Ever

Ultimately, academic catchphrases like "public-facing scholarship" don't quite capture the reality of the situation that requires the sort of "religion for realists" I've been advocating in this book. The phrase is too casual and too neutral. We need to see our work as active prebunking and debunking. Unlike experts trying to stop the spread of online myths about COVID-19 vaccines or the 2020 presidential election, we find ourselves working against disinformation that is held by a majority of the population, not a vocal minority. The fact is, citizens throughout the Western world are already convinced they know how religion works and how it connects to their own social, economic, and political behavior. This is because there is no shortage of parents, pastors, pundits, politicians, pollsters, and yes, professors who reproduce Anglo-Protestant misconceptions. Our task isn't merely "public-facing scholarship," but active engagement in inoculating citizens from disinformation and tackling misconceptions head on.

This doesn't mean our scientific quest is to "debunk" supernatural claims or replace religion itself. I'm in agreement with sociologists Rodney Stark and Roger Finke who argued, "As social scientists, our purpose should neither be to discredit religion nor to advance a religion of science. Rather, our fundamental quest is to apply social scientific tools to the relationship between human beings and what they experience as divine."[10] And I would add, our perpetual challenge is to help people see why this is important and beneficial to us all.

Ironically, the group that benefits the most from maintaining Anglo-Protestant misconceptions are the interest groups and actors who already understand quite well how religion works. Instead of depending on the rational beliefs of devout Americans (which would require coherent argumentation and consistent principles), they surreptitiously appeal to their identities, stoking ethnonationalist and partisan outrage cloaked in the talk of "worldviews" and "religious freedom." Similarly, such groups carefully articulate their strategies for religious growth mostly with the language of "culture" and the victory of world-transforming ideas. Yet their growing focus on promoting fertility and patriarchal gender roles while restricting immigration betrays their clear understanding that words like "religion" and "culture" imply "ethnoculture." And population dynamics hold the key to its future. To be sure, Anglo-Protestant assumptions have long stressed the importance of individual freedom and rights, a priority that must still be communicated up front. Yet actors on the Christian far-right are warming to the idea that their perpetual political and cultural influence will require the control of institutions. This includes education and all branches of government.

For the foreseeable future, religion will continue to shape the West. But in centering Anglo-Protestant cultural elements like faith, ideas, and agency, we misunderstand how religion will do so. Like people in Indiana Jones's world, we go about life oblivious to the evidence that "the gods" work differently than how we've always understood. The evidence-based, scientific study of religion must go public.

But it takes more than Indiana Jones. It takes resources in the form of grant money for data, funding lines for tenure-track scholars, professional recognition for the highest quality work, guidelines for implementing open science standards, and intentional training for effective public scholarship. And all these possibilities start with enough people, embedded in institutions, becoming convinced that there is a need. This book is a plea to those people. Now more than ever, there *is* a need.

Notes

Introduction

1. Just so readers know, I've put a lot of thought into this. Dr. Jones is a tenured professor at Marshall College, a fictional school. In the most recent film, he retires in 1969 from Hunter College in New York City. The fact that he's not placed at an Ivy League university (à la Robert Langdon in Dan Brown's novels) or even his alma mater, the University of Chicago, suggests that his notoriety as a professor isn't central to the story line. In a world where institutional prestige signals professional worth, he's a nobody. From what we see in the classroom, his students are bored. And those who are interested in him are more attracted to his hottie-professor appearance than his harrowing research and breathtaking discoveries. He's overwhelmed with grading and administrative responsibilities, so much so that he sneaks out the window of his dusty office to avoid students clamoring for help. In both situations where he's asked to weigh-in as an archeological expert, he's the second choice, only asked when the first choices are dead or kidnapped. And he has little research funding to speak of, apparently depending on resources from the local museum, where his buddy Marcus is the curator.
2. Thomas and Thomas (1928).
3. This is something Auguste Comte, whom many consider the founder of sociology, actually proposed. Though he believed the metaphysical claims of religion were false, he proposed replacing its useful social niche with a "religion of humanity" complete with rituals, saints, and sacred holidays (Bourdeau 2023).
4. There is, in fact, a long history of religion specialists lamenting (and often demonstrating) how their research is marginalized within their particular discipline (Fox 2021; Grzymala-Busse 2012; Kettell 2024; Mills 1983; Prothero 2008; Rios and Roth 2020).
5. See the debates about definitions of religion in Hughes and McCutcheon (2021).
6. Harari (2015); Hughes and McCutcheon (2021); Riesebrodt (2010); Smith (2017); but see Stark and Finke (2000).
7. Brauer (2018); Davis et al. (2023); Inglehart (2020); Stone (2020); Voas and Chaves (2016).
8. Durkheim (1995 [1912]); Haidt (2012); Harari (2015).
9. Wilson (2023).
10. Blankholm (2022).
11. Taves (2009).
12. Perry and Davis (2024).
13. Perry (2022, 2023a).
14. Among some exceptions to this trend, see Ammerman (2020, 2021); Vasquez (2011).
15. James Davison Hunter (2010) describes these foundational assumptions well for American Christians, but I would argue it extends to the broader culture in terms of how we think about religion.
16. Blankholm (2022).

17. Ammerman (2020, 2021); Bellah (1970:216–228); Hughes and McCutcheon (2021); Riesebrodt (2010); Vasquez (2011).
18. Djupe et al. (2023).
19. Brauer (2018); Churchill, Ugur, and Yew (2017); Franck and Iannaccone (2014); Gill and Lundsgaarde (2004); Halla et al. (2016); Olson et al. (2020); Stone (2020).
20. Perry (2023b, 2023c).

Chapter 1

1. I write about this movement and my own experiences with adoption in my first book, *Growing God's Family* (see Perry 2017).
2. For a book-length example of this perspective, see Joyce (2013).
3. This quote has appeared on numerous CAFO materials, but a recent instance can be found at: https://cafo.org/old-summit/about-summit/.
4. Brinton and Bennett (2015).
5. Perry (2017:129–130).
6. Hayford and Morgan (2008); Perry and Schleifer (2019).
7. Conservative Christian leaders recognize infertility and other physical barriers can hinder childbearing. Yet they are also quite consistent in their view that childlessness is a sad fate and childlessness by choice is a sign of selfishness and rejection of God's plan for couples (e.g., Nielson 2013; Piper 2020; Wilson 2013).
8. Cruver (2010).
9. Frankfurt (2005); C. Mills (1940).
10. McKinnon (2022); Snow and Machalek (1984).
11. Stark and Finke (2000:92). Italics theirs.
12. Hunter (2010); Perry (2017).
13. Butler (2021); Du Mez (2020); Perry (2019); Tisby (2019).
14. In 2013 data provided by the Christian polling firm Barna Group (2013), Americans who say they have confessed their sins and trusted Jesus as their savior were not statistically distinguishable from other Americans in the percentage who had adopted, nor were those who say the Bible is completely true in all that it teaches (see Perry 2017:60).
15. Perry and Schleifer (2019).
16. Stone (2023).
17. I've excluded several regions from which Americans have never adopted a relatively significant number of children such as Europe, South America, or Australia.
18. Schaefer Riley (2019).

Chapter 2

1. Haidt (2012); Tajfel (1982).
2. Mason (2018).
3. For a survey of these insights, see Haidt (2006: Chapter 1).
4. Bardon (2020); Evans (2003); Greene (2013): Haidt (2012); Kahneman (2011).
5. Haidt (2012).
6. Lewis, MacGregor, and Putnam (2013); Lim and Putnam (2010); Putnam and Campbell (2010:473).
7. Lichterman (1992).
8. Bardon (2020).
9. C. Smith (2003).
10. Ammerman (2020, 2021); Bellah (1970:216–228); Bender, Cadge, and Smilde (2013); Lichterman (2013); Smilde and May (2015); Vasquez (2011).

11. Chaves (2010).
12. Caluori et al. (2020); Epley et al. (2009); Feuerbach (1845); Jackson et al. (2018); Niebuhr (1929); Ross et al. (2012); Spinoza (2002).
13. Perry et al. (2024).
14. Perry (2019: 76–79).
15. Hawkins (2021); Niebuhr (1929); Noll (2006).
16. Hadaway, Marler, and Chaves (1993, 1998); Presser and Stinson (1998).
17. For example, people are less likely to affirm overtly racist answers to questions, even if it's how they really feel. Or they may be less likely to affirm statements that would embarrass them, like about their pornography use or homosexual thoughts or genitals. This understandable human tendency is one of the key reasons scholars have gravitated toward big data analytics where we're observing behavior when you assume we're not looking rather than your direct answers. Instead of asking whether people are willing to date members of another race, we can just look at how people set up their own dating profiles on Match.com and whether they initiate dates with people of another race or even respond to invitations (spoiler: people are more prejudiced in their dating habits than we'd be led to believe from their direct answers). Instead of asking persons in a region of the country how much pornography they watch, we can just look at Google Trends data for how often people search for words like "free porn," "xxx," "lesbian porn," and so on (spoiler: For some reason, those searches seem to be higher in regions with lots of evangelicals and churchgoers). See Lundquist and Lin (2015); Stephens-Davidowitz (2014); Whitehead and Perry (2018).
18. Brenner (2011, 2012, 2016); Brenner and DeLamater (2014).
19. Franzen and Griebel (2013).
20. Malley (2004).
21. Perry and McElroy (2020).
22. Allport (1954:446).
23. Al-Kire et al. (2024); Devos and Mohamed (2014).
24. These are all numbers I calculated from the General Social Surveys, which are publicly available.
25. McCarty (2019); Mason (2018). For a helpful popular treatment on this subject, see Klein (2020). And an excellent book about how our geographic mobility has contributed to growing polarization is Bill Bishop's (2009) *The Big Sort*.
26. Brauer (2018); Voas and Chaves (2016).
27. Mason (2018); Perry (2022, 2023a).
28. Braunstein (2022); Campbell, Layman, and Green (2020); Campbell et al. (2018); Djupe et al. (2018); Egan (2020); Hout and Fischer (2002; 2014); Margolis (2018a, 2018b); Patrikios (2008).
29. G. Smith (2021).
30. Durkheim (1995 [1912]).
31. Willer (2009).
32. Coe and Chapp (2017).
33. Pew asked Americans what religion they thought President Trump was in the American Trends Panel Wave 61 in February 2020 and asked what religion they thought Biden was in the American Trends Panel Wave 84 in March 2021. I am comparing responses from the two surveys, not from the same survey.
34. Paxton (2004:42).
35. Al-Kire et al. (2024).
36. For the sources of each quote, see Perry (2023a).
37. Perry (2023a).

Chapter 3

1. C. Smith (2007). Smith acknowledges that other religions also contain many of these elements (though the salubrious emotional benefits he describes certainly seem tailored to Christian theology), and he does not draw a hard distinction between conservative or liberal expressions of Christianity.
2. Harris (2004); Pinker (2018: Chapter 22).
3. Pew Research Center (2015b, 2017b).
4. Pew Research Center (2015a).
5. The Amish teaching on the role of good works in one's salvation may strike many Protestants as heterodox, but these views are not uniform across the Amish.
6. Amish Studies Center at Elizabethtown College (2023).
7. Hunter (2010); Perry (2017).
8. Hatch (1989).
9. Rand (1999:39).
10. Bardon (2020).
11. Finke and Stark (2005); Stark and Finke (2000).
12. Hout, Greeley, and Wilde (2001).
13. Lindsay (2007); Perry (2019).
14. Stone (2022).
15. Perry and Schleifer (2019).
16. Riess (2019).
17. Pew Research Center (2015b).
18. Inglehart (2020); Norris and Inglehart (2011).
19. The percentage of Americans who identify as Catholic since 1948 has remained relatively flat, according to data from Gallup (see: https://news.gallup.com/poll/1690/religion.aspx).
20. Pew Research Center (2015b, 2017a).
21. Kaufmann, Goujon, and Skirbekk (2012); Skirbekk, Kaufmann, and Goujon (2010).
22. Pew Research Center (2022).
23. Brauer (2018).
24. Voas (2009).
25. Bardon (2020); Bellah (1970:216–228); Haidt (2012).
26. Stolz (2020); Molteni and Biolcati (2023); Uecker and Bowman (2024).
27. Kiley and Vaisey (2020); Underwood et al. (2022); Vaisey and Lizardo (2016).
28. Bengtson et al. (2017); McPhail (2019); Voas (2003).
29. Stone (2020).
30. Molteni and Biolcati (2023).
31. Brauer (2018). See also Voas and Chaves (2016).
32. Wiertz and Lim (2021); Olson et al. (2020).
33. Schnabel and Bock (2017).
34. Gervais and Najle (2018).
35. Dunson (2021); Walker (2021); Wilson (2023); Wolfe (2022: Chapter 5).
36. Dawkins (1989).
37. DeYoung (2020).
38. Butler (2023); Gurry (2024).
39. Stone (2022).
40. Stone (2023).

Chapter 4

1. Sehat (2016).
2. Giddens (1984).

3. Pew Research Center (2022).
4. Bruce and Voas (2023).
5. See a survey of these views in Stark and Finke (2000: Introduction).
6. See surveys in Stolz (2020); Stone (2020).
7. Broćić and Miles (2021).
8. Mayrl and Oeur (2009); Perry, Baker, and Grubbs (2021); Roos (2014).
9. In a 2015 survey of 1,500 evangelical and Black Protestant pastors, over 75% of respondents said they refer church members to a professional counselor when the situation requires more than two sessions (see: https://www.thearda.com/data-archive?fid=PASVY15&tab=2).
10. Perry (2024a); Weber (1978:428).
11. Gallup (2024); Jones (2021); Perry (2024a); Rosenfeld, Thomas, and Hausen (2019).
12. Franck and Iannaccone (2014); Gill and Lundsgaarde (2004); Immerzeel and van Tubergen (2013); Stone (2020).
13. Immerzeel and van Turbergen (2013); Norris and Inglehart (2011); Lee and Suh (2017); Storm (2017).
14. Iannaccone (1992); Iyer (2016); Stone (2020:42).
15. Ruiter and van Tubergen (2009); van Ingen and Moor (2015).
16. Chaves and Eagle (2016).
17. Franck and Iannaccone (2014); Kose, Kuka, and Shenhav (2021); Schmick (2023).
18. Jones (2017).
19. This is from the 1709 translation by William Reeves.
20. Stolz, Pollack, and De Graaf (2020); Stolz et al. (2021).
21. Froese (2004); Yang (2011).
22. Francis-Tan (2023).
23. Pew Research Center (2015b); Yang (2011).
24. Justin Long's analysis is shown in Lee (2014).
25. Madison, *The Writings*, Volume 8 (see https://oll.libertyfund.org/title/madison-the-writings-vol-8-1808-1819); Finke and Stark (2005); Stone (2020).
26. Stolz et al. (2020, 2021).
27. Çokgezen and Hussen (2021).
28. Barro, Hwang, and McCleary (2010); Chaves et al. (1994); Fox and Breslawski (2023); Gill (1999); Grim and Finke (2007, 2010); Koev (2023).
29. Pew Research Center (2009); Grim and Finke (2007, 2010); Saiya and Manchanda (2020).
30. On China's score on Pew's GRI and SHI indexes, see Pew Research Center (2009:28). For studies documenting the link between religious regulation and lower religious adherence or religiosity, see Barro et al. (2010); Chaves and Cann (1992); Chaves et al. (1994); Çokgezen and Hussen (2021); Fox and Tabory (2008); North and Gwin (2004); Ridge (2020); Ruiter and van Tubergen (2009). For cases with mixed findings, see Francis-Tan (2023); McCleary and Barro (2006); and Driessen (2014).
31. Çokgezen (2022); Chaves et al. (1994); Fox and Breslawski (2023); Ridge (2020).
32. Drelichman, Vidal-Robert, and Voth (2021).
33. Scholars like Northmore-Ball and Evans (2016); Rosta (2020); and Pollack and Rosta (2017) have come to identical conclusions with different data sets.
34. These numbers come from both Pew's 2015 survey of eastern Europe that I've referenced in Figures 4.4. and 4.5. as well as their 2015 Global Attitudes Survey of multiple nations.
35. Huang and Cha (2020); Perry et al. (2023); Pew Research Center (2019a); Reinhart (2018); Swift (2017).

36. Rosta (2020).
37. Baker et al. (2020); Perry et al. (2022b); Whitehead et al. (2018).
38. Gorski and Perry (2022); Perry et al. (2022a).

Chapter 5

1. Rios and Roth (2020).
2. Bardon (2020); Dromi and Stabler (2023); Grossman (2021).
3. Berger (1963:176); Grossmann (2021).
4. Funnily enough, even our decision to pursue a life of research in the academy is quite often the path our close relatives have chosen. Allison Morgon and her colleagues (2022) show that tenure-track faculty are up to 25 times more likely to have a parent with a PhD. They also find that rate nearly doubles at prestigious universities.
5. Coley (2018); O'Brien (2017).
6. Gerth and Mills (1946:156).
7. Devendorf et al. (2023).
8. Altenmuller et al. (2021).
9. Blanton and Krasnicki (2024); Ecklund (2010); Gross and Simmons (2009).
10. Rios and Roth (2020).
11. In their survey of graduate students at elite sociology programs in the United States, Blanton and Krasnicki (2024) find among the leading predictors of choosing religion as an area of research is being personally religious. Conversely, the leading predictor of finding religion irrelevant is being personally irreligious.
12. Perry (2023b, 2023c).
13. Scheitle and Ecklund (2018) and Barnes et al. (2020). Negative perceptions related to religion and scientific rigor take place at the institutional level as well. Business professor Mathew Isaac and his colleagues (2021) used a series of experiments to show that overtly religious advertisements hurt the scientific reputations of religious universities. Regardless of the religious beliefs of scientists at those institutions or their work, the assumption was that hints of institutional religious commitment meant their intentions were indoctrination rather than honest science.
14. Rios et al. (2015).
15. Lewis and Sekaquaptewa (2016).
16. Barnes et al. (2020).
17. Wallace et al. (2014); Wright et al. (2013).
18. See Neil Gross's (2013) discussion of audit studies to assess anti-conservative bias in academia.
19. Rivera (2012).
20. Barnes et al. (2020); Scheitle and Dabbs (2021).
21. Becker (1963).
22. Blanton and Krasnicki (2024).
23. National Center of Education Statistics data from 2020. American Council on Education data from 2017.
24. Grossmann (2021).
25. Blanton and Krasnicki (2024).
26. Scheitle, Remsburg, and Platt. (2021).
27. Henrich, Heine, and Norenzayan (2010).
28. Haidt (2012).
29. Grossmann (2021:3).

Chapter 6

1. Perry (2024b); Pew Research Center (2024).
2. Barnes et al. (2020); Stark and Finke (2000:21); Yancey (2011); Yancey, Reimer, and O'Connell (2015).
3. Bardon (2020); Greene (2013); Haidt (2012); Kahan (2017).
4. Lee (2021); O'Brien and Noy (2020).
5. Funk (2020); Jones (2018); Pew Research Center (2019b).
6. Kozlowski (2022); Mann and Schleifer (2020).
7. Evans (2018); Harris (2010); Pinker (2018).
8. Gauchat and Andrews (2018); Lee (2021); O'Brien and Noy (2020); Scheitle (2018).
9. Perry (2023c).
10. Stark and Finke (2000:21).

References

Achen, Christopher, and Larry Bartels. 2016. *Democracy for Realists: Why Elections Do Not Produce Responsive Government*. Princeton, NJ: Princeton University Press.

Al-Kire, Rosemary L., Chad A. Miller, Michael H. Pasek, Samuel L. Perry, and Clara L. Wilkins. 2024. "White by another name? Can anti-Christian bias claims serve as a racial dog whistle?" *Psychological Science* 35(4): 415–434.

Allport, Gordon W. 1954. *The Nature of Prejudice*. New York: Addison-Wesley.

Altenmuller, Marlene S., Leonie Lucia Lange, and Mario Gollwitzer. 2021. "When research is me-search: How researchers' motivation to pursue a topic affects laypeople's trust in science." *PLoS One* 16(7): e0253911.

Amish Studies Center at Elizabethtown College. 2023. https://groups.etown.edu/amishstudies/. Accessed May 4, 2023.

Ammerman, Nancy T. 2020. "Rethinking religion: Toward a practice approach." *American Journal of Sociology* 126(1): 6–51.

Ammerman, Nancy T. 2021. *Studying Lived Religion: Contexts and Practices*. New York: NYU Press.

Baker, Joseph O., Samuel L. Perry, and Andrew L. Whitehead. 2020. "Keep America Christian (and white): Christian nationalism, fear of ethnoracial outsiders, and intention to vote for Donald Trump in the 2020 presidential election." *Sociology of Religion* 81(3): 272–293.

Bardon, Adrian. 2020. *The Truth about Denial: Bias and Self-Deception in Science, Politics, and Religion*. New York: Oxford University Press.

Barna Group. 2013. *Becoming Home: Adoption, Foster Care, and Mentoring—Living Out God's Heart for Orphans*. Grand Rapids, MI: Zondervan.

Barnes, M. Elizabeth, Jasmine M. Truong, Daniel Z. Grunspan, and Sara E. Brownell. 2020. "Are scientists biased against Christians? Exploring real and perceived bias against Christians in academic biology." *PLoS One* 15(1): e0226826.

Barro, Robert, Jason Hwang, and Rachel McCleary. 2010. "Religious conversion in 40 countries." *Journal for the Scientific Study of Religion* 49(1): 15–36.

Becker, Howard. 1963. *Outsiders: Studies in the Sociology of Deviance*. New York: Simon & Schuster.

Bellah, Robert N. 1970. *Beyond Belief: Essays on Religion in a Post-Traditional World*. New York: Harper & Row.

Bender, Courtney, Wendy Cadge, Peggy Levitt, and David Smilde, eds. 2013. *Religion on the Edge: De-Centering and Re-Centering the Sociology of Religion*. New York: Oxford University Press.

Bengston, Vern L., Norella M. Putney, and Susan C. Harris. 2013. Faith and Families: How Religion Is Passed Down across Generations. New York: Oxford University Press.

Berger, Peter. 1963. Invitation to Sociology: A Humanist Perspective. New York: Doubleday.

Bishop, Bill. 2009. The Big Sort: Why the Clustering of Like-Minded America Is Tearing Us Apart. New York: Houghton Mifflin Harcourt.

Blankholm, Joseph. 2022. The Secular Paradox: On the Religiosity of the Not Religious. New York: NYU Press.

Blanton, Matthew, and Daniel Krasnicki. 2024. "'Value-conditioned interest': Secularity, institutional support, and the sociology of religion in graduate departments." Sociological Quarterly 65(3): 401–423.

Bourdeau, Michel. 2023. "August Comte." In Stanford Encyclopedia of Philosophy, edited by Edward N. Zalta and Uri Nodelman. https://plato.stanford.edu/entries/comte/#SocDouSta. Accessed March 31, 2024.

Brauer, Simon. 2018. "The surprising predictable decline of religion in the United States." Journal for the Scientific Study of Religion 57(4): 654–675.

Braunstein, Ruth. 2022. "A theory of political backlash: Assessing the religious right's effects on the religious field." Sociology of Religion 83(3): 293–323.

Brenner, Philip S. 2011. "Identity importance and the overreporting of religious service attendance: Multiple imputation of religious attendance using the American Time Use Study and the General Social Survey." Journal for the Scientific Study of Religion 50(1): 103–115.

Brenner, Philip S. 2012. "Overreporting of voting participation as a function of identity." Social Science Journal 49(4): 421–429.

Brenner, Philip S. 2016. "Lies, damned lies, and survey self-reports? Identity as a cause of measurement bias." Social Psychology Quarterly 79(4): 333–354.

Brenner, Philip S., and John D. DeLamater. 2014. "Social desirability bias in self-reports of physical activity: Is an exercise identity the culprit?" Social Indicators Research 117: 489–504.

Brinton, Sara, and Amanda Bennett. 2015. In Defense of the Fatherless: Redeeming International Adoption and Orphan Care. Glasgow, Scotland: Christian Focus.

Broćić, Miloš, and Andrew Miles. 2021. "College and the 'culture war': Assessing higher education's influence on moral attitudes." American Sociological Review 86(5): 856–895.

Bruce, Steve, and David Voas. 2023. "Secularization vindicated." Religions 14(3): 301.

Butler, Anthea. 2021. White Evangelical Racism: The Politics of Morality in America. Chapel Hill: University of North Carolina Press.

Butler, Joshua Ryan. 2023. "The ethics of contraception." https://joshuaryanbutler.com/blog/the-ethics-of-contraception/. Accessed May 4, 2023.

Caluori, Nava, Joshua Conrad Jackson, Kurt Gray, and Michele Gelfand. 2020. "Conflict Changes How People View God." Psychological Science 31(3): 280–292.

Campbell, David E., Geoffrey C. Layman, and John C. Green. 2020. Secular Surge: A New Fault Line in American Politics. Cambridge: Cambridge University Press.

Campbell, David E., Geoffrey C. Layman, John C. Green, and Nathanael G. Sumaktoyo. 2018. "Putting politics first: The impact of politics on American religious and secular orientations." American Journal of Political Science 62(3): 551–565.

Chaves, Mark. 2010. "SSSR presidential address rain dances in the dry season: Overcoming the religious congruence fallacy." Journal for the Scientific Study of Religion 49(1): 1–14.

Chaves, Mark, and David E. Cann. 1992. "Regulation, pluralism, and religious market structure: Explaining religion's vitality." Rationality and Society 4(3): 272–290.

Chaves, Mark, and Alison J. Eagle. 2016. "Congregations and social services: An update from the third wave of the National Congregations Study." Religions 7(5): 55.

Chaves, Mark, Peter J. Schraeder, and Mario Sprindys. 1994. "State regulation of religion and Muslim religious vitality in the industrialized West." Journal of Politics 56(4): 1087–1097.

Churchill, Sefa Awaworyi, Mehmet Ugur, and Siew Ling Yew. 2017. "Government education expenditures and economic growth: A meta-analysis." BE Journal of Macroeconomics 17(2): 20160109.

Coe, Kevin, and Christopher B. Chapp. 2017. "Religious rhetoric meets the target audience: Narrowcasting faith in presidential elections." Communication Monographs 84(1): 110–127.

Çokgezen, Murat. 2022. "Can the state make you more religious? Evidence from Turkish experience." Journal for the Scientific Study of Religion 61(2): 349–373.

Çokgezen, Murat, and Mohammed Seid Hussen. 2021. "The impact of government interference to religion on religious giving: Evidence from European countries." VOLUNTAS: International Journal of Voluntary and Nonprofit Organizations 32: 414–429.

Coley, Jonathan S. 2018. Gay on God's Campus: Mobilizing for LGBT Equality at Christian Colleges and Universities. Chapel Hill: University of North Carolina Press.

Cruver, Dan. 2010. "Adoption, adoption, and caring for orphans." Together for Adoption, November 15. www.togetherforadoption.org.

Davis, Jim, Michael Graham, and Ryan Burge. 2023. The Great Dechurching: Who's Leaving, Why Are They Going, and What Will It Take to Bring Them Back? Grand Rapids, MI: Zondervan.

Dawkins, Richard. 1989. The Selfish Gene. 2nd ed. New York: Oxford University Press.

Devendorf, Andrew R., Sara E. Victor, Jonathan Rottenberg, Rose Miller, Stephen P. Lewis, Jennifer J. Muehlenkamp, and Dese'Rae L. Stage. 2023. Stigmatizing our own: Self-relevant research (me-search) is common but frowned upon in clinical psychological science. Clinical Psychological Science 11(6): 1122–1140.

Devos, Thierry, and Hafsa Mohamed. 2014. "Shades of American identity: Implicit relations between ethnic and national identities." Social and Personality Psychology Compass 8(12): 739–754.

DeYoung, Kevin. 2020. "It's time for a new culture war strategy." The Gospel Coalition. https://www.thegospelcoalition.org/blogs/kevin-deyoung/its-time-for-a-new-culture-war-strategy/. Accessed May 4, 2023.

Djupe, Paul A., Andrew R. Lewis, and Anand E. Sokhey. 2023. The Full Armor of God: The Mobilization of Christian Nationalism in American Politics. Cambridge: Cambridge University Press.

Djupe, Paul A., Jacob R. Neiheisel, and Kimberly H. Conger. 2018. "Are the politics of the Christian right linked to state rates of the nonreligious? The importance of salient controversy." Political Research Quarterly 71(4): 910–922.

Donnermeyer, Joseph F. 2015. "Doubling time and population increase of the Amish." Journal of Amish and Plain Anabaptist Studies 3: 94–109.

Drelichman, Mauricio, Jordi Vidal-Robert, and Hans-Joachim Voth. 2021. "The long-run effects of religious persecution: Evidence from the Spanish Inquisition." Proceedings of the National Academy of Sciences 118(33): e2022881118.

Driessen, Michael D. 2014. "Regime type, religion-state arrangements, and religious markets in the Muslim world." Sociology of Religion 75(3): 367–394.

Dromi, Shai M., and Samuel D. Stabler. 2023. Moral Minefields: How Sociologists Debate Good Science. Chicago, IL: University of Chicago Press.

Du Mez, Kristin Kobes. 2020. Jesus and John Wayne: How White Evangelicals Corrupted a Faith and Fractured a Nation. New York: Liveright.

Dunson, Ben C. 2021. "Don't rejoice in the collapse of cultural Christianity." First Things. https://www.firstthings.com/web-exclusives/2021/08/dont-rejoice-in-the-collapse-of-cultural-christianity. Accessed May 4, 2023.

Durkheim, Emile. 1995 [1912]. The Elementary Forms of Religious Life. New York: The Free Press.

Ecklund, Elaine Howard. 2010. Science vs. Religion: What Scientists Really Think. Oxford University Press.

Egan, Patrick J. 2020. "Identity as dependent variable: How Americans shift their identities to align with their politics." American Journal of Political Science 64(3): 699–716.

Epley, Nicholas, Benjamin A. Converse, Alexa Delbosc, George A. Monteleone, and John T. Cacioppo. 2009. "Believers' estimates of God's beliefs are more egocentric than estimates of other people's beliefs." PNAS 106(51): 21533–21538.

Evans, John H. 2018. Morals Not Knowledge: Recasting the Contemporary US Conflict between Religion and Science. Berkeley: University of California Press.

Evans, Jonathan St BT. 2003. "In two minds: Dual-process accounts of reasoning." Trends in Cognitive Sciences 7(10): 454–459.

Feuerbach, Ludwig. 1845. The Essence of Christianity. Amherst, NY: Prometheus.

Finke, Roger, and Rodney Stark. 2005. The Churching of America, 1776–2005: Winners and Losers in Our Religious Economy. New Brunswick, NJ: Rutgers University Press.

Fox, Jonathan. 2021. "Religion as an overlooked element of international relations." International Studies Review 3(3): 53–73.

Fox, Jonathan, and Jori Breslawski. 2023. "State support for religion and government legitimacy in Christian-majority countries." American Political Science Review 117(4): 1395–1409.

Fox, Jonathan, and Ephraim Tabory. 2008. "Contemporary evidence regarding the impact of state regulation of religion on religious participation and belief." Sociology of Religion 69(3): 245–271.

Francis-Tan, Andrew. 2023. "Economy of shadows: The effects of restrictive regulation on religiosity in China." Journal for the Scientific Study of Religion 62(3): 624–647.

Franck, Raphaël, and Laurence R. Iannaccone. 2014. "Religious decline in the 20th century West: Testing alternative explanations." Public Choice 159: 385–414.

Frankfurt, Harry G. 2005. On Bullshit. Princeton, NJ: Princeton University Press.

Franzen, Aaron B., and Jenna Griebel. 2013. "Understanding a cultural identity: The confluence of education, politics, and religion within the American concept of biblical literalism." Sociology of Religion 74(4): 521–543.

Froese, Paul. 2004. "Forced secularization in Soviet Russia: Why an atheistic monopoly failed." Journal for the Scientific Study of Religion 43(1): 35–50.

Funk, Cary. 2020. "Key findings about Americans' confidence in science and their views on scientists' role in society." https://www.pewresearch.org/fact-tank/2020/02/12/key-findings-about-americans-confidence-in-science-and-their-views-on-scientists-role-in-society/. Pew Research Center. Accessed March 25, 2023.

Gallup. 2024. "How religious are Americans?" https://news.gallup.com/poll/358364/religious-americans.aspx. Accessed on June 26, 2024.

Gauchat, Gordon W., and Kenneth T. Andrews. 2018. "The cultural-cognitive mapping of scientific professions." American Sociological Review 83(3): 567–595.

Gerth, H. H., and C. Wright Mills. 1946. From Max Weber: Essays in Sociology. New York: Oxford University Press.

Gervais, Will M., and Maxine B. Najle. 2018. "How many atheists are there?" Social Psychological and Personality Science 9(1): 3–10.

Giddens, Anthony. 1984. The Constitution of Society: Outline of the Theory of Structuration. Berkeley, CA: University of California Press.

Gill, Anthony. 1999. "Government regulation, social anomie and protestant growth in Latin America: A cross-national analysis." Rationality and Society 11(3): 287–316.

Gill, Anthony, and Erik Lundsgaarde. 2004. "State welfare spending and religiosity: A cross-national analysis." Rationality and Society 16(4): 399–436.

Gorski, Philip S., and Samuel L. Perry. 2022. The Flag and the Cross: White Christian Nationalism and the Threat to American Democracy. New York: Oxford University Press.

Greene, Joshua. 2013. Moral Tribes: Emotion, Reason, and the Gap between Us and Them. New York: Penguin.

Grim, Brian J., and Roger Finke. 2007. "Religious persecution in cross-national context: Clashing civilizations or regulated religious economies?" American Sociological Review 72(4): 633–658.

Grim, Brian J., and Roger Finke. 2010. The price of freedom denied: Religious persecution and conflict in the twenty-first century. Cambridge, UK: Cambridge University Press.

Gross, Neil. 2013. Why Are Professors Liberal and Why Do Conservatives Care? Cambridge, MA: Harvard University Press.

Gross, Neil, and Solon Simmons. 2009. "The religiosity of American college and university professors." Sociology of Religion 70 (2): 101–29.

Grossmann, Matt. 2021. How the Social Sciences Got Better. New York: Oxford University Press.

Grzymala-Busse, Anna. 2012. "Why comparative politics should take religion (more) seriously." Annual Review of Political Science 15: 421–42.

Gurry, Peter. 2024. "How the pill obscures God's truth in creation." https://www.the gospelcoalition.org/. Accessed April 1, 2024.

Hadaway, C. Kirk, Penny Long Marler, and Mark Chaves. 1993. "What the polls don't show: A closer look at U.S. Church Attendance." American Sociological Review 58(6): 741–752.

Hadaway, C. Kirk, Penny Long Marler, and Mark Chaves. 1998. "Overreporting church attendance in America: Evidence that demands the same verdict." American Sociological Review 63(1): 122–130.

Haidt, Jonathan. 2006. The Happiness Hypothesis: Finding Modern Truth in Ancient Wisdom. New York: Basic Books.

Haidt, Jonathan. 2012. The Righteous Mind: Why Good People Are Divided by Politics and Religion. New York: Vintage.

Halla, Martin, Mario Lackner, and Johann Scharler. 2016. "Does the welfare state destroy the family? Evidence from OECD member countries." Scandinavian Journal of Economics 118(2): 292–323.

Harari, Yuval Noah. 2015. Sapiens: A Brief History of Humankind. New York: Harper.

Harris, Sam. 2004. The End of Faith: Religion, Terror, and the Future of Reason. New York: Norton.

Harris, Sam. 2010. The Moral Landscape: How Science Can Determine Human Values. New York: Simon and Schuster.

Hatch, Nathan O. 1989. The Democratization of American Christianity. New Haven, CT: Yale University Press.

Hawkins, J. Russell. 2021. The Bible Told Them So: How Southern Evangelicals Fought to Preserve White Supremacy. New York: Oxford University Press.

Hayford, Sarah R., and S. Philip Morgan. 2008. "Religiosity and fertility in the United States: The role of fertility intentions." Social Forces 86(3): 1163–1188.

Henrich, Joseph, Steven J. Heine, and Ara Norenzayan. 2010. "The weirdest people in the world?" Behavioral and Brain Sciences 33(2–3): 61–83.

Hout, Michael, and Claude S. Fischer. 2002. "Why more Americans have no religious preference: Politics and generations." American Sociological Review 67(2): 165–190.

Hout, Michael, and Claude S. Fischer. 2014. "Explaining why more Americans have no religious preference: Political backlash and generational succession, 1987–2012." Sociological Science 1: 423–447.

Hout, Michael, Andrew Greeley, and Melissa J. Wilde. 2001. "The demographic imperative in religious change in the United States." American Journal of Sociology 107(2): 468–500.

Huang, Christine, and Jeremiah Cha. 2020. "Russia and Putin receive low ratings globally." Pew Research Center. https://www.pewresearch.org/fact-tank/2020/02/07/russia-and-putin-receive-low-ratings-globally/. Accessed May 2, 2022.

Hughes, Aaron W., and Russell T. McCutcheon. 2021. What Is Religion? Debating the Academic Study of Religion. New York: Oxford University Press.

Hunter, James Davison. 2010. To Change The World: The Irony, Tragedy, and Possibility of Christianity in the Late Modern World. New York: Oxford University Press.

Iannaccone, Laurence R. 1992. "Religious markets and the economics of religion." Social Compass 39(1): 123–131.

Immerzeel, Tim, and Frank Van Tubergen. 2013. "Religion as reassurance? Testing the insecurity theory in 26 European countries." European Sociological Review 29(2): 359–372.

Inglehart, Ronald F. 2020. Religion's Sudden Decline: What's Causing It, and What Comes Next? New York: Oxford University Press.

Isaac, Mathew S., Carl Obermiller, and Rebecca Jen-Hui Wang. 2021. "The downside of divinity? Reputational harm to sectarian universities from overtly religious advertising." Journal of Advertising 50(4): 423–440.

Iyer, Sriya. 2016. "The new economics of religion." Journal of Economic Literature 54(2): 395–441.

Jackson, Joshua Conrad, Neil Hester, and Kurt Gray. 2018. "The faces of God in America: Revealing religious diversity across people and politics." PLoS ONE 13(6): e0198745.

Jones, Jeffrey M. 2017. "Parent Income, Degree, Religion Key Factors in School Choices." Gallup. https://news.gallup.com/poll/217247/school-choices-vary-parent-religion-education-income.aspx. Accessed June 21, 2024.

Jones, Jeffrey M. 2018. "Confidence in higher education down since 2015." Gallup. https://news.gallup.com/opinion/gallup/242441/confidence-higher-educat ion-down-2015.aspx?g_source=link_newsv9&g_campaign=item_248492&g_ medium=copy. Accessed March 22, 2023.

Jones, Jeffrey M. 2021. "U.S. church membership falls below majority for first time." Gallup. https://news.gallup.com/poll/341963/church-membership-falls-below-majority-first-time.aspx#:~:text=Story%20Highlights&text=WASHING TON%2C%20D.C.%20%2D%2D%20Americans'%20membership,2018%20 and%2070%25%20in%201999. Accessed May 5, 2023.

Joyce, Kathryn. 2013. The Child Catchers: Rescue, Trafficking, and the New Gospel of Adoption. New York: Public Affairs.

Kahan, Dan M. 2017. "Misconceptions, misinformation, and the logic of identity-protective cognition." Cultural Cognition Project Working Paper Series No. 164. Yale Law & Economics Research Paper. https://ssrn.com/abstract=2973067.

Kahneman, Daniel. 2011. Thinking, Fast and Slow. New York: Farrar, Straus, and Giroux.

Kaufmann, Eric, Anne Goujon, and Vegard Skirbekk. 2012. "The end of secularization in Europe? A socio-demographic perspective." Sociology of Religion 73(1): 69–91.

Kettell, Steven. 2024. "Is political science (still) ignoring religion? An analysis of journal publications, 2011–2020." PS: Political Science and Politics 57(1): 64–69.

Kiley, Kevin, and Stephen Vaisey. 2020. "Measuring stability and change in personal culture using panel data." American Sociological Review 85(3): 477–506.

Klein, Ezra. 2020. Why We're Polarized. New York: Simon and Schuster.

Koev, Dan. 2023. "The influence of state favoritism on established religions and their competitors." Politics and Religion 16(1): 129–159.

Kose, Esra, Elira Kuka, and Na'ama Shenhav. 2021. "Women's suffrage and children's education." American Economic Journal: Economic Policy 13(3): 374–405.

Kozlowski, Austin C. 2022. "How conservatives lost confidence in science: The role of ideological alignment in political polarization." Social Forces 100(3): 1415–1443.

Lee, Chengpang, and Myungsahm Suh. 2017. "State building and religion: Explaining the diverged path of religious change in Taiwan and South Korea, 1950–1980." American Journal of Sociology 123(2): 465–509.

Lee, John J. 2021. "Party polarization and trust in science: What about democrats?" Socius 7. https://doi.org/10.1177/23780231211010101

Lee, Morgan. 2014. "Sorry, Tertullian." Christianity Today. https://www.christianitytoday.com/ct/2014/december/sorry-tertullian.html. Accessed May 5, 2023.

Lewis, Neil A., Jr., and Denise Sekaquaptewa. 2016. "Beyond test performance: A broader view of stereotype threat." Current Opinion in Psychology 11: 40–43.

Lewis, Valerie A., Carol Ann MacGregor, and Robert D. Putnam. 2013. "Religion, networks, and neighborliness: The impact of religious social networks on civic engagement." Social Science Research 42(2): 331–346.

Lichterman, Paul. 1992. "Self-help reading as a thin culture." Media, Culture and Society 14(3): 421–447.

Lichterman, Paul. 2013. "Studying public religion: Beyond the beliefs-driven actor." Pages 115–136 in Religion on the Edge, edited by Courtney Bender, Wendy Cadge, and David Smilde. New York: Oxford University Press.

Lim, Chaeyoon, and Robert D. Putnam. 2010. "Religion, social networks, and life satisfaction." American Sociological Review 75(6): 914–933.

Lindsay, D. Michael. 2007. Faith in the Halls of Power: How Evangelicals Joined the American Elite. New York: Oxford University Press.

Lundquist, Jennifer H., and Ken-Hou Lin. 2015. "Is love (color) blind? The economy of race among gay and straight daters." Social Forces 93(4): 1423–1449.

Malley, Brian. 2004. How the Bible Works: An Anthropological Study of Evangelical Biblicism. New York: Altamira.

Mandryk, Jason. 2010. Operation World: The Definitive Prayer Guide to Every Nation. Downers Grove, IL: InterVarsity Press.

Mann, Marcus, and Cyrus Schleifer. 2020. "Love the science, hate the scientists: Conservative identity protects belief in science and undermines trust in scientists." Social Forces 99(1): 305–332.

Margolis, Michele F. 2018a. From Politics to the Pews: How Partisanship and the Political Environment Shape Religious Identity. Chicago: Chicago University Press.

Margolis, Michele F. 2018b. "How politics affects religion: Partisanship, socialization, and religiosity in America." Journal of Politics 80(1): 30–43.

Mason, Lilliana. 2018. Uncivil Agreement: How Politics Became Our Identity. Chicago, IL: University of Chicago Press.

Mayrl, Damon, and Freeden Oeur. 2009. "Religion and higher education: Current knowledge and directions for future research." Journal for the Scientific Study of Religion 48(2): 260–275.

McCarty, Nolan. 2019. Polarization: What Everyone Needs to Know. New York: Oxford University Press.

McCleary, Rachel M., and Robert J. Barro. 2006. "Religion and Political Economy in an International Panel." Journal for the Scientific Study of Religion 45(2): 149–175.

McKinnon, Andrew M. 2022. "The sociology of conversion narratives: A conundrum, a theory, and an opportunity." Journal of Contemporary Religion 37(1): 89–105.

McPhail, Brian L. "Religious heterogamy and the intergenerational transmission of religion: A cross-national analysis." Religions 10(2): 109.

Mills, C. Wright. 1940. "Situated actions and vocabularies of motive." American Sociological Review 5(6): 904–913.

Molteni, Francesco, and Ferruccio Biolcati. 2023. "Religious decline as a population dynamic: Generational replacement and religious attendance in Europe." Social Forces 101(4): 2034–2058.

Morgan, Allison C., Nicholas LaBerge, Daniel B. Larremore, Mirta Galesic, Jennie E. Brand, and Aaron Clauset. 2022. "Socioeconomic roots of academic faculty." Nature Human Behaviour 6: 1625–1633.

Muller, Friedrich Max. 1870. An Introduction to the Science of Religion. London: Longman, Greens.

Niebuhr, H. Richard. 1929. The Social Sources of Denominationalism. New York: Henry Holt.

Nielson, Kathleen. 2013. "The problem of the childfree life." The Gospel Coalition. https://www.thegospelcoalition.org/article/the-problem-with-the-childfree-life/. Accessed May 6, 2013.

Noll, Mark A. 2006. The Civil War as a Theological Crisis. Chapel Hill: University of North Carolina Press.

Norris, Pippa, and Ronald Inglehart. 2011. Sacred and Secular: Religion and Politics Worldwide. Cambridge: Cambridge University Press.

North, Charles M., and Carl R. Gwin. 2004. "Religious freedom and the unintended consequences of state religion." Southern Economic Journal 71(1): 103–117.

Northmore-Ball, Ksenia, and Geoffrey Evans. 2016. "Secularization versus religious revival in eastern Europe: Church institutional resilience, state repression and divergent paths." Social Science Research 57: 31–48.

O'Brien, John. 2017. Keeping It Halal: The Everyday Lives of Muslim American Teenage Boys. Princeton, NJ: Princeton University Press.

O'Brien, Timothy L., and Shiri Noy. 2020. "Political identity and confidence in science and religion in the United States." Sociology of Religion 81(4): 439–461.

Patrikios, Stratos. 2008. "American Republican religion? Disentangling the causal link between religion and politics in the US." Political Behavior 30(3): 367–389.

Paxton, Robert O. 2004. The Anatomy of Fascism. New York: Knopf.

Perry, Samuel L. 2017. Growing God's Family: The Global Orphan Care Movement and the Limits of Evangelical Activism. New York: NYU Press.

Perry, Samuel L. 2019. Addicted to Lust: Pornography in the Lives of Conservative Protestants. New York: Oxford University Press.

Perry, Samuel L. 2022. "American religion in the era of increasing polarization." Annual Review of Sociology 48: 87–107.

Perry, Samuel L. 2023a. "Mating call, dog whistle, trigger: Asymmetric alignments, race, and the use of reactionary religious rhetoric in American politics." Sociological Theory 41(1): 56–82.

Perry, Samuel L. 2023b. "(Why) is the sociology of religion marginalized? Results from a survey experiment." American Sociologist 54: 485–511.

Perry, Samuel L. 2023c. "Religion matters (and doesn't go away when sociologists ignore it)." Sociological Forum 38(4): 1456–1463.

Perry, Samuel L. 2024a. "Falling Trust, Expertise, and Appeal: America's Changing Views on Clergy." Pre-print. http://osf.io/mrwx7/download

Perry, Samuel L. 2024b. "Sociology and Its (Limited) Publics: The Case of 'Christian Nationalism'." The American Sociologist. https://doi.org/10.1007/s12 108-024-09627-1

Perry, Samuel L., Joseph O. Baker, and Joshua B. Grubbs. 2021. "Ignorance or culture war? Christian nationalism and scientific illiteracy." Public Understanding of Science 30(8): 930–946.

Perry, Samuel L., and Joshua T. Davis. 2024. "What makes politicians 'religious'? How identity congruence shapes religious evaluations." Journal for the Scientific Study of Religion 63(1): 137–159.

Perry, Samuel L., Joshua B. Grubbs, and Cyrus Schleifer. 2024. "In our own image: How Americans rate Jesus on the ideological spectrum." Review of Religious Research 66(2) 157–176.

Perry, Samuel L., and Elizabeth E. McElroy. 2020. "Does the Bible tell me so? Weighing the influence of content versus bias on Bible interpretation using survey experiments." Journal for the Scientific Study of Religion 59(4): 569–585.

Perry, Samuel L., Sarah Riccardi-Swartz, Joshua T. Davis, and Joshua B. Grubbs. 2023. "The religious right and Russia: Christian nationalism and Americans' views on Russia and Vladimir Putin before and after the Ukrainian invasion." Journal for the Scientific Study of Religion 62(2): 439–450.

Perry, Samuel L., and Cyrus Schleifer. 2019. "Are the faithful becoming less fruitful? The decline of conservative protestant fertility and the growing importance of religious practice and belief in childbearing in the US." Social Science Research 78: 137–155.

Perry, Samuel L., Andrew L. Whitehead, and Joshua B. Grubbs. 2022a. "'I don't want everybody to vote': Christian nationalism and restricting voter access in the United States." Sociological Forum, 37(1): 4–26.

Perry, Samuel L., Andrew L. Whitehead, and Joshua B. Grubbs. 2022b. "The devil that you know: Christian nationalism and intent to change one's voting behavior for or against Trump in 2020." Politics and Religion 15(2): 229–246.

Pew Research Center. 2009. "Global restrictions on religion." https://www.pewresea rch.org/religion/2009/12/17/global-restrictions-on-religion/. Accessed May 5, 2023.

Pew Research Center. 2015a. "America's changing religious landscape." file:///C:/ Users/admin/Downloads/RLS-08-26-full-report%20(7).pdf. Accessed May 4, 2023.

Pew Research Center. 2015b. "The future of world religions: Population growth projections, 2010–2015." https://www.pewresearch.org/religion/2015/04/02/ religious-projections-2010-2050/. Accessed May 4, 2023.

Pew Research Center. 2017a. "Europe's growing Muslim population." file:///
C:/Users/admin/Downloads/FULL-REPORT-FOR-WEB-POSTING.pdf.
Accessed May 4, 2023.

Pew Research Center. 2017b. "The changing global religious landscape." https://
www.pewresearch.org/religion/2017/04/05/the-changing-global-religi
ous-landscape/#:~:text=The%20number%20of%20Christians%20is%20pr
ojected%20to%20rise%20by%2034,3.1%20billion%2C%20or%2032%25).
Accessed May 4, 2023.

Pew Research Center. 2019a. "Climate change and Russia are partisan flashpoints
in public's views of global threats." https://www.pewresearch.org/politics/2019/
07/30/climate-change-and-russia-are-partisan-flashpoints-in-publics-views-
of-global-threats/#growing-partisan-divides-in-views-of-russia. Accessed May
2, 2022.

Pew Research Center. 2019b. "The growing partisan divide in views of higher education." https://www.pewresearch.org/social-trends/2019/08/19/the-grow
ing-partisan-divide-in-views-of-higher-education-2/. Accessed March 22, 2023.

Pew Research Center. 2022. "Modeling the future of religion in America." file:///C:/
Users/admin/Downloads/US-Religious-Projections_FOR-PRODUCTION-
9.13.22.pdf. Accessed May 4, 2023.

Pew Research Center. 2024. "8 in 10 Americans say religion is losing influence in
public life." https://www.pewresearch.org/religion/2024/03/15/8-in-10-americ
ans-say-religion-is-losing-influence-in-public-life/. Accessed April 2, 2024.

Pinker, Steven. 2018. Enlightenment now: The Case for Reason, Science,
Humanism, and Progress. New York: Penguin.

Piper, John. 2020. "Are Christian couples required to have kids?" https://www.desi
ringgod.org/interviews/are-christian-couples-required-to-have-kids. Accessed
May 6, 2023.

Pollack, Detlef, and Gergely Rosta. 2017. Religion and Modernity: An International
Comparison. New York: Oxford University Press.

Presser, Stanley, and Linda Stinson. 1998. "Data collection mode and social desirability bias in self-reported religious attendance." American Sociological Review
63(1): 137–145.

Prothero, Stephen R. 2008. Religious Literacy: What Every American Needs to
Know—And Doesn't. San Francisco, CA: HarperOne.

Putnam, Robert D., and David E. Campbell. 2010. American Grace: How Religion
Divides and Unites Us. New York: Simon and Schuster.

Olson, Daniel V.A., Joey Marshall, Jong Hyun Jung, and David Voas. 2020. "Sacred
canopies or religious markets? The effect of county-level religious diversity
on later changes in religious involvement." Journal for the Scientific Study of
Religion 59(2): 227–246.

Rand, Ayn. 1999. The Return of the Primitive: The Anti-Industrial Revolution.
New York: Meridian.

Reinhart, R. J. 2018. "Republicans more positive on U.S. relations with Russia."
Gallup. https://news.gallup.com/poll/237137/republicans-positive-relations-
russia.aspx. Accessed May 5, 2023.

Ridge, Hannah M. 2020. "State regulation of religion: The effect of religious
freedom on Muslims' religiosity." Religion, State and Society 48(4): 256–275.

Riesebrodt, Martin. 2010. The Promise of Salvation: A Theory of Religion. Chicago, IL: University of Chicago Press.

Riess, Jana. 2019. "The incredible shrinking Latter-Day Saint family." Salt Lake City Tribune. https://www.sltrib.com/religion/2019/06/15/commentary-incredible/. Accessed May 4, 2023.

Rios, Kimberly, Zhen Hadassah Cheng, Rebecca R. Totton, and Azim F. Shariff. 2015. "Negative stereotypes cause Christians to underperform in and disidentify with science." Social Psychological and Personality Science 6(8): 959–967.

Rios, Kimberly, and Zachary C. Roth. 2020. "Is 'me-search' necessarily less rigorous research? Social and personality psychologists' stereotypes of the psychology of religion." Self and Identity (7): 825–840.

Rivera, Lauren A. 2012. "Hiring as cultural matching: The case of elite professional service firms." American Sociological Review 77(6): 999–1022.

Roos, J. Micah. 2014. "Measuring science or religion? A measurement analysis of the National Science Foundation sponsored science literacy scale 2006–2010." Public Understanding of Science 23(7): 797–813.

Rosenfeld, Michael J., Reuben J. Thomas, and Sonia Hausen. 2019. "Disintermediating your friends: How online dating in the United States displaces other ways of meeting." Proceedings of the National Academy of Sciences 116(36): 17753–17758.

Ross, Lee D., Yphtach Lelkes, and Alexandra G. Russell. 2012. "How Christians reconcile their personal political views and the teachings of their faith: Projection as a means of dissonance reduction." PNAS 109(10): 3616–3622.

Rosta, Gergely. 2020. "Hungary: Continuing and changing trends and mechanisms of religious change." Pages 99–117 in Religiosity in East and West: Conceptual and Methodological Challenges from Global and Local Perspectives. Springer.

Ruiter, Stijn, and Frank Van Tubergen. 2009. "Religious attendance in cross-national perspective: A multilevel analysis of 60 countries." American Journal of Sociology 115(3): 863–95.

Saiya, Nilay, and Stuti Manchanda. 2020. "Anti-conversion laws and violent Christian persecution in the states of India: A quantitative analysis." Ethnicities 20(3): 587–607.

Schaefer Riley, Naomi. 2019. "Christians are pro-life after birth, too." Wall Street Journal. https://www.wsj.com/articles/christians-are-pro-life-after-birth-too-11560465692. Accessed May 3, 2023.

Scheitle, Christopher P. 2018. "Politics and the perceived boundaries of science: Activism, sociology, and scientific legitimacy." Socius 4. https://doi.org/10.1177/2378023118769544

Scheitle, Christopher P., and Ellory Dabbs. 2021. "Religiosity and identity interference among graduate students in the sciences." Social Science Research 93: 102503.

Scheitle, Christopher P., and Elaine Howard Ecklund. 2018. "Perceptions of religious discrimination among U.S. scientists." Journal for the Scientific Study of Religion 57(1): 139–155.

Scheitle, Christopher P., Taylor Remsburg, and Lisa F. Platt. 2021. "Science graduate students' reports of discrimination due to gender, race, and religion: Identifying shared and unique predictors." Socius 7. https://doi.org/10.1177/2378023121 1025183.

Schmick, Ethan. 2023. "The determinants of early investments in urban school systems in the United States." Education Finance and Policy. https://doi.org/10.1162/edfp_a_00403

Schnabel, Landon, and Sean Bock. 2017. "The persistence and exceptional intensity of American religion: A response to recent research." Sociological Science 4: 636–700.

Sehat, David. 2016. The Myth of American Religious Freedom. Updated Edition. New York: Oxford University Press.

Skirbekk, Vegard, Eric Kaufmann, and Anne Goujon. 2010. "Secularism, fundamentalism, or Catholicism? The religious composition of the United States to 2043." Journal for the Scientific Study of Religion 49(2): 293–310.

Smilde, David, and Matthew May. 2015. "Causality, normativity, and diversity in 40 years of US sociology of religion: Contributions to paradigmatic reflection." Sociology of Religion 76(4): 369–388.

Smith, Christian. 2003. Moral, Believing Animals: Human Personhood and Culture. New York: Oxford University Press.

Smith, Christian. 2007. "Why Christianity works: An emotions-focused phenomenological account." Sociology of Religion 68(2): 165–178.

Smith, Christian. 2017. Religion: What It Is, How It Works, and Why It Matters. Princeton, NJ: Princeton University Press.

Smith, Gregory A. 2021. "More white Americans adopted than shed evangelical label during Trump presidency, especially his supporters." https://www.pewresearch.org/fact-tank/2021/09/15/more-white-americans-adopted-than-shed-evangelical-label-during-trump-presidency-especially-his-supporters/. Accessed February 25, 2023.

Snow, David A., and Richard Machalek. 1984. "The sociology of conversion." Annual Review of Sociology 10(1): 167–190.

Spinoza, Baruch. 2002. Spinoza: Complete Works. Edited by Michael L. Morgan. New York: Hackett Publishing.

Stark, Rodney, and Roger Finke. 2000. Acts of Faith: Explaining the Human Side of Religion. Berkeley: University of California Press.

Stephens-Davidowitz, Seth. 2014. "The cost of racial animus on a Black candidate: Evidence using Google search data." Journal of Public Economics 118: 26–40.

Stolz, Jorg. 2020. "Secularization theories in the twenty-first century: Ideas, evidence, and problems." Sociology Compass 67(2): 282–308.

Stolz, Jorg, Detlef Pollack, and Nan Dirk De Graaf. 2020. "Can the state accelerate the secular transition? Secularization in East and West Germany as a natural experiment." European Sociological Review 36(4): 626–642.

Stolz, Jorg, Detlef Pollack, Nan Dirk De Graaf, and Jean-Philippe Antonietti. 2021. "Losing my religion as a natural experiment: How state pressure and taxes led to church disaffiliations between 1940 and 2010 in Germany. Journal for the Scientific Study of Religion 60(1): 83–102.

Stone, Lyman. 2018. "How long until we're all Amish?" Medium. https://medium.com/migration-issues/how-long-until-were-all-amish-268e3d0de87. Accessed May 4, 2023.

Stone, Lyman. 2020. "Promise and peril: The history of American religiosity and its recent decline." American Enterprise Institute. https://www.aei.org/wp-content/uploads/2020/04/Promise-and-Peril.pdf. Accessed May 3, 2023.

Stone, Lyman. 2022. "America's growing religious-secular fertility divide." Institute for Family Studies. https://ifstudies.org/blog/americas-growing-religious-secular-fertility-divide. Accessed May 4, 2023.

Stone, Lyman. 2023. "The Truth About Demographic Decline." https://lawliberty.org/forum/the-truth-about-demographic-decline/. Accessed August 25, 2023.

Storm, Ingrid. 2017. "Does economic insecurity predict religiosity? Evidence from the European Social Survey 2002-2014. Sociology of Religion 78(2): 146-172.

Swift, Art. 2017. "Putin's image rises in the U.S., mostly among Republicans." Gallup. https://news.gallup.com/poll/204191/putin-image-rises-mostly-among-republicans.aspx. Accessed May 5, 2023.

Tajfel, Henri, ed. 1982. Social Identity and Intergroup Relations. Cambridge: Cambridge University Press.

Taves, Ann. 2009. Religious Experience Reconsidered: A Building-Block Approach to the Study of Religion and Other Special Things. Princeton, NJ: Princeton University Press.

Thomas, William Isaac, and Dorothy Swaine Thomas. 1928. The Child in America: Behavior Problems and Programs. New York: Knopf.

Tisby, Jemar. 2019. The Color of Compromise: The Truth about the American Church's Complicity in Racism. Grand Rapids, MI: Zondervan.

Uecker, Jeremy E., and Carl Desportes Bowman. 2024. "Still soul searching? Remapping adolescent religious commitment." Sociology of Religion 85(2): 197-218.

Underwood, Ted, Kevin Kiley, Wenyi Shang, and Stephen Vaisey. 2022. "Cohort succession explains most change in literary culture." Sociological Science 9: 184-205.

Vaisey, Stephen, and Omar Lizardo. 2016. "Cultural fragmentation or acquired dispositions? A new approach to accounting for patterns of cultural change." Socius 2. https://doi.org/10.1177/2378023116669726

van Ingen, Erik, and Nienke Moor. 2015. "Explanations of changes in church attendance between 1970 and 2009." Social Science Research 52: 558-569.

Vásquez, Manuel A. 2011. More than Belief: A Materialist Theory of Religion. New York: Oxford University Press.

Voas, David. 2003. "Intermarriage and the demography of secularization." British Journal of Sociology 54(1): 83-108.

Voas, David. 2009. "The rise and fall of fuzzy fidelity in Europe." European Sociological Review 25(2): 155-168.

Voas, David, and Mark Chaves. 2016. "Is the United States a counterexample to the secularization thesis?" American Journal of Sociology 121(5): 1517-1556.

Walker, Andrew T. 2021. "What we lose in the decline of cultural Christianity." The Gospel Coalition. https://www.thegospelcoalition.org/article/decline-cultural-christianity/. Accessed May 4, 2023.

Wallace, Michael, Bradley R. E. Wright, and Allen Hyde. 2014. "Religious affiliation and hiring discrimination in the American South: A field experiment." Social Currents 1(2): 189-207.

Weber, Max. 1978. Economy and Society: An Outline of Interpretive Sociology. Vol. 2. Berkeley, CA: University of California Press.

Wiertz, Dingeman, and Chaeyoon Lim. 2021. "The rise of the nones across the United States, 1973 to 2018: State-level trends of religious affiliation and participation in the general social survey." Sociological Science 8: 429–454.

Whitehead, Andrew L., and Samuel L. Perry. 2018. "Unbuckling the Bible belt: A state-level analysis of religious factors and Google searches for porn." Journal of Sex Research 55(3): 273–283.

Whitehead, Andrew L., Samuel L. Perry, and Joseph O. Baker. 2018. "Make America Christian again: Christian nationalism and voting for Donald Trump in the 2016 presidential election." Sociology of Religion 79(2): 147–171.

Willer, Robb. 2009. "Groups reward individual sacrifice: The status solution to the collective action problem." American Sociological Review 74(1): 23–43.

Wilson, Douglas. 2013. "Childfree by choice?" https://www.youtube.com/watch?v=zmbaXdbP_CI. Accessed May 6, 2023.

Wilson, Douglas. 2023. Mere Christendom. Moscow, ID: Canon.

Wolfe, Stephen. 2022. The Case for Christian Nationalism. Moscow, ID: Canon.

Wright, Bradley R. E., Michael Wallace, John Bailey, and Allen Hyde. 2013. "Religious affiliation and hiring discrimination in New England: A field experiment." Research in Social Stratification and Mobility 34: 111–126.

Yancey, George. 2011. Compromising Scholarship: Religious and Political Bias in American Higher Education. Waco, TX: Baylor University Press.

Yancey, George, Sam Reimer, and Jake O'Connell. 2015. "How academics view conservative protestants." Sociology of Religion 76(3): 315–336.

Yang, Fenggang. 2011. Religion in China: Survival and Revival under Communist Rule. New York: Oxford University Press.

Yinger, J. Milton. 1970. The Scientific Study of Religion. New York: Macmillan.

Index